Christmas, 1970

To Virginia —
Who has
many of me
joy.

D0427451

E llen

AS FAR AS
I CAN STEP

AS FAR AS
I CAN STEP

Virginia Law

WORD BOOKS, Publisher
Waco, Texas • London, England

TO
MOTHER AND DAD
WHO GUIDED MY FIRST
PHYSICAL AND SPIRITUAL STEPS

CONTENTS

AS FAR AS
I CAN STEP

I.

"BURLEIGH IS DEAD"

"BURLEIGH IS DEAD!"

I knew he was even before I went to answer the telephone.

"Yes, he is! Burleigh is dead," was the only explanation for the telephone's ring that I could possibly give to Mother as I sat across the breakfast table from her that morning in Tallahassee, Florida.

Strange. Just as if a video tape was running in my mind, I remembered a long forgotten incident. I was hearing a famous Nazarene preacher. Uncle Bud Robinson was an uneducated man with little polished English or pulpit grace. Yet he had a keen way of expressing himself, using earthy illustrations and parables. In his unique lisping tongue he was speaking of the shocking experiences and difficult times in life. He lifted his left hand and cupped the fingers. Then dramatically he appeared to pick up something and put it into his cupped hand as he stammered, "T-t-t-the Lord, He lifts you up and p-p-puts you in the hollow of His hand."

11

Cupping his right hand over the left, he said, "H-h-he p-p-puts the other hand on top, 'nnn you ain't got no bisness stickin y'or head out."

This scene was in my mind as I answered my father's call to the telephone. On the phone was Dr. Melvin Blake, Secretary for Africa at the New York office of the Methodist Missions Board. Before he could speak I said, "Melvin, Burleigh is dead, isn't he?"

"Yes," he told me, "Burleigh has been killed by a Congolese rebel soldier. That's all the details the State Department can give us at this time."

As I turned back from the telephone, I had the strangest sense of peace. This nightmarish experience still seemed to be all around me, yet somehow it didn't quite touch me. Deep inside me I found I was supported by a conviction so powerful it seemed to come from outside of my self. I knew, "All things work together for good" (Rom. 8:28, KJV), and this reality gripped me. Here was something I could hold to. A spot where I could let down my weight.

Yet, *Burleigh was dead!* How could this be possible? And I was still alive. How could such a part of me be dead?

I left the phone to enter the embrace of my nineteen-year-old son David. Eleven-year-old Margaret Ann joined us as we wept together.

There were so many questions.

"Was Burleigh shot?"

"Wonder if it was a poison arrow?"

"Do you suppose he was tortured?"

Yet above all these questions came the thought, *This is no tragedy. Tragedy just couldn't happen to Burleigh Law. A life that had known the fulfillment and joy with adventure that Burleigh knew couldn't end in tragedy. No matter what!*

David sat for a long time thinking over the *where* and *how.* Then he looked up and said, "Mom, I know Dad died as a Christian. The soldier will never forget that."

Suddenly I realized that there was nothing Burleigh could possibly have left to his nineteen-year-old son that would have been a greater heritage.

Immediately we faced a decision—would we let Paul know? Paul was just finishing a summer school session and still had a few exams left. We would interrupt these if we phoned him now. There was nothing he could do, yet we wanted and needed the support of this seventeen-year-old member of our family. Were we selfish in our desire to call him?

We decided that we were. Instead we called his principal. As soon as Paul's exams were over he would let us know. I would then tell him.

Amazing how many decisions we had to reach even though we did not have a body to bury. Friends came rushing over. The phone rang constantly. It was all so strange until I could not realize that this was actually I, Virginia Law, facing this experience.

Alone in my room that night I sat remembering. When had it all begun? Perhaps way back in my childhood. I had dreamed of the kind of man I wanted someday to marry. As a freshman in college I met Burleigh. On our very first date, while we were riding across the Kentucky hills, I had turned to him and said, "This is the greatest day of my life." It had been. Burleigh answered my girlhood dream.

Burleigh came into my life at the point when I was discovering my own identity. His life became intertwined with what I knew as "Me." He felt called to be a missionary. I chose my major, Elementary Education, because as the wife of a missionary I would need to teach our children. Any professional ambitions I might have had were lost in my desire to be Burleigh's wife. I was challenged to make my contribution to the world through him. God had a great work for Burleigh to do. I was excited to be a part of it.

As we sought this plan of God for our lives, Burleigh

was a part of my faith in God and my religious experiences. I felt that he was the most deeply dedicated young man I had ever known. His expression of his faith permeated every part of his life.

On our first date, there was a tremendous feeling of purpose and meaning when he shared with me his dreams. As we returned to the dorm, Burleigh reached over and took my hand and prayed. He thanked God for the marvelous time we had had together and for the things we had in common. Then he asked God to bless our lives as we enjoyed each other. This became a dating ritual for us. Since then God had blessed us with twenty-two years to enjoy each other.

What an exciting life we had lived! Only ten days before I had returned stateside for a five-week vacation. I planned to return to Congo, Africa, where we had been serving as missionaries for fifteen years. Yet in the midst of all the excitement there had always been Burleigh. Quiet, calm, confident Burleigh. He was the stabilizing element in my life. What adventure! There stood this very masculine Burleigh, giving me a sense of physical security in the midst of danger. I felt safe. What problems? I could lean upon Burleigh with his unfaltering faith in God.

How could I separate myself from this person who had become a part of me? My adult self-image, my whole feeling of personhood had been fulfilled in this man. I felt free to express myself. I was free to see and laugh at life. I was free to venture. All this because of the love and support of this man who called me to be the woman I could become. My greatest talents and my true area of self-expression came forward as we created our home. Being his wife and the mother of his children had given me my sense of creative expression. I had never wished for any other.

Remembering this I looked up. There on my dresser was a row of pill bottles.

"Something to make you sleep—something to help you,"

my friends had said as they handed me the tranquilizers. Now these seemed to say to me, "Life is more than you can take."

I knew there was no earthly way that I could brace up. I could never humanly accept this terrible shaking event. I could not fight life. I could not fight against the hurt. Nothing could protect me from annihilation, from the destruction of everything that had been Virginia. A part of me had died. The terrible hopelessness of my situation, the futility of anything that I could do, began to overwhelm me. I was fighting a whirlpool in a swift flood. I cried out for help.

"Virginia, you have to give up," came a comforting inner conviction. "You have to surrender, you can't fight it. Yet you do have a choice in your surrender. You can give in to grief and take tranquilizers, or you can simply surrender to God and go forward by His grace."

As I knelt by my bed, I could not phrase a prayer. I could only cry out, "Father, I surrender to your love. I do love you. Long ago I made that decision and nothing now changes that fact. I don't want to fight. I don't want to resist. I won't try to hold on to Burleigh. Thank you, Father, for letting me have him for these twenty-two years."

I relaxed on the conviction that all things work together for good to those who love God.

"Father," I prayed, "I do believe that You will work this out for good. I don't see how this could be. I don't understand why I believe it—but I do."

Somehow, quietly, I did believe. It couldn't be otherwise for Burleigh. But what about me? My entire life was shattered. I had never dreamed of being anything other than Burleigh Law's wife. His death would destroy me, and I could feel that destruction in my anguish.

"Don't let *me* be the tragedy that happens, Father. Let me become a part of that good."

Peace quietly flooded my heart. My tears ebbed. I knelt resting my head on the bed while my heart was bathed in comfort. Again I prayed, "Father, I surrender Burleigh—my grief—myself."

The tenseness and strain left. Finally I slipped into bed. I do not remember when my head hit the pillow. I was immediately asleep.

Early the next morning I awoke while the house was quiet. The fact of Burleigh's death began to return. Yet, at the same time I was aware of a very real Presence in the room. My thoughts were pushed out by other thoughts which moved in and overpowered mine. I knew that I was communicating with God through this invasion of His Spirit.

"Virginia, you can't understand now. Even if I explained it all you couldn't understand. You just have to have faith. Believe that Burleigh's death will be used more than would twenty years added to his life."

My heart embraced this comfort. I lay meditating. Should I be asking "Why?" My heart seemed to cry out again and again, "Why, Why?"

"This is a normal question to ask," I found coming to me. "You must admit your doubts. Faith always operates against the questions and doubts in life. If you don't have these, you don't need faith. You believe, not because you don't have doubts but despite them."

"But, if . . ." I said. "If Burleigh had come home with me . . . If we had not gone back to Congo in 1962 . . . If Burleigh had taken a job and we had stayed in America . . . If Burleigh had not been where the rebels came . . . If the arrow had missed or the gun misfired."

"The 'ifs' like the 'whys' you must commit in faith to me," the Spirit said.

Somehow I had found the strength I needed to commit Burleigh into God's loving care and purpose. Yet I felt more keenly my own loss. I could feel myself being crushed and torn assunder. Even to dimly think of a tomorrow without Burleigh was more than I could face. *Gone* was the person to whom I belonged. Gone forever was Love and all it had brought into my life.

"Father, I can't face life without Burleigh's love."

"But Virginia," the Spirit whispered, "love did not begin with Burleigh and it doesn't end with him. God loved you before you knew Burleigh. He loved you while you had Burleigh. He still loves you. You will find love in the heart of every Christian if you will just keep your heart open to receive it."

If you will keep your heart open. The words kept burning themselves into my mind. So soon I could feel myself closing up. I felt hurt and bleeding, actual physical pain. Every person reminded me of something that was painful to remember. I was tempted to withdraw and not face these memories.

As I lay thinking, I remembered an incident that happened when Paul was only two years old. He accidently jerked a hot iron onto his arm and the iron burned its imprint into second and third degree burns. We rushed him to the hospital where he was treated and bandaged. As we took him home the doctor gave us a quart of medication. "Keep the bandage soaked," he told us. "Don't let it get dry day or night. If you can keep this arm from scabbing over, he won't have any scars."

For the next few days we carefully followed his instructions. During the night we would set the alarm and get up to wet the bandage. We began to see tiny bead-like cells appearing. Then a plastic-thin film covered the burn. Finally we recognized normal skin. Today there is only one small scar where despite our efforts a scab formed.

"If you don't scab, you won't scar," was the message to me out of this memory. Keeping my heart open was the painful condition that I must work at through the next months, even years, if I were to find my life saved from being a bleak, lonely road

There were still my three children to consider. Life had to go on for them especially, I knew. *But where can I take hold? What can I do?* Any idea of where to turn or what to do seemed beyond my imagination.

Go to Scarritt College in Nashville, Tennessee, came into my mind as a command. I lay there stunned. I had never been to Nashville. I did not know anyone at Scarritt. Yet the idea would not be quieted. There was no question about it. I knew that this was my guidance for that moment. Today as I look back, I can recount all the reasons that made this such a wise decision, but at that moment I was not capable of thinking wisely. I only knew I must follow directions. Although it was not yet 5:00 A.M., I arose and went out to the typewriter. The stillness of the morning was broken by the clatter of typewriter keys spelling out:

> Yesterday I received word that my husband, Burleigh Law, had been killed by rebel soldiers in Congo. Feeling the need to become involved in something creative, I would like to enroll in Scarritt College this fall . . .

Often I would look back upon that morning for comfort and for reassurance that God was guiding. But nothing changed the fact, "Burleigh is dead."

II.

SMILING WITH A PINK ROSE

"PAT IS ON THE PHONE, Virginia. She wants you to come down to the shop and let her set your hair for the memorial service."

Oh, no, was my immediate reaction, *I don't want my hair set.*

This was Friday morning. Planning a memorial service was proving difficult. We had received the word on Thursday that Burleigh had been killed in Congo by a rebel soldier. This morning, a cablegram had come saying that Burleigh had been buried at Wembo Nyama, Congo. Neither the children nor I would ever be interested in trying to bring his body back to America. His heart had been in Congo— there was the place to leave him buried.

We did want a Memorial Service, however, "Nothing sad," was the request of each of the children. "Let it be a service of praise and thanksgiving for Dad."

But to go have my hair set suddenly seemed to be taking the idea of praise and thanksgiving too far.

Fortunately, before I answered the offer, the thought suddenly occured to me, "If Pat came bringing a lemon pie, you would gladly accept this expression of her concern. But Pat doesn't have time for that. This is her way of offering you her love."

"All right," was the answer I gave out loud. "Tell her I'll go."

When I arrived at the beauty parlor the next day I noticed a pretty pink rosebud on Pat's table. Pat picked it up and began to pin it on my shoulder. "Knowing you as I do," she said, "I'm sure you feel that you have been honored by Burleigh's death. I wanted to get a bright red one but had to settle for this pink. White just wouldn't be right."

As I sat under the dryer, the rose began to take on even more meaning to me. I would have expected Pat to feel that my loss was a real tragedy; yet here was just a casual acquaintance voicing for me the way I really felt deep within my heart.

I began to think about the memorial service. Many of the plans were already made. The congregation was to sing "O God, Our Help in Ages Past." Then Burleigh's favorite song was to be the closing solo—"How Great Thou Art." The tone of the service was already one of joy and praise but I wanted it to be even more so. How could this be done? There under the dryer I had an idea.

When I reached home I called David, Paul, and Margaret Ann into my room and told them about my rosebud corsage. Then I explained my unusual desire, "I want to wear a red corsage to the memorial service and I want each of you children to wear a small red flower. If Dad had been promoted to some higher position in government we would wear a flower in his honor. What higher position is there anywhere than to become a martyr in Christian service?"

David spoke up immediately. "Mother, you can do anything you want, just like you want, today and from now on.

You don't have to prove to anyone that you loved Burleigh Law. . . . I think it's a good idea."

And so I ordered two red corsages and three single red carnations. At the same time I requested that the flowers used in the church be red and white.

"I need to run down town to the Hat Shoppe for a few minutes," my Mother said, later that day. "I don't have a thing in black."

"Well, you don't need a thing in black," I answered.

"What should I wear then?" she asked.

"What other dress could you wear?"

"I could wear my white one," she said.

"Then why not wear your pretty red straw hat with it?"

Mother looked at me trying to decide if I were really serious.

"Burleigh would love the red hat. I'll bet if he could come in right now and pick out a hat for you to wear, he'd take that one."

For several moments Mother stood thinking. Slowly a smile began to form around her mouth. "You know, I think he would, too."

Early on the Sunday of the service the children and I were sitting together on the big bed talking. Remembering Congo, Paul asked, "How did the graduation at Katubwe High School go?" He and David had a childhood friend, Kasongo, who was to graduate. Kasongo was the son of Burleigh's foreman. The three little boys had grown up together playing around where their daddies were working.

"It was great. Dad flew down for it and took Wemb'ula with him."

"Boy, I'll bet that was a real thrill for him. He'd never been that far from home before."

"Yes, it was. And a thrill for Dad, too. He had always wanted to do something really nice for Papa Wemb'ula and this was a chance."

As we sat remembering this faithful workman, I suddenly remembered something else.

"You know what Dad asked me when he came home? He wanted to know if I could match up any more pairs of socks like I had given away. You boys remember all those socks you left in Congo?"

"Yeah."

"Well, I divided them up among your friends. On Sunday morning Dad was asked to sit on the platform for the bacculareate service. He crossed his knees and happened to notice that although he had on two brown socks, one of them had a yellow design on it and the other a red one. Then he looked across the stage and there sat Kasongo with his knees crossed; he also had on one brown sock with a yellow design and one brown one with red. The mates to Dad's socks!"

At that we all broke into laughter. For several years Burleigh had battled to keep his socks matched and in his own drawer. His best socks had a way of ending up in his two sons' supply. Just to think that even months after they had left Congo their dad was still fighting the problem of keeping his socks matched brought back a flood of humorous memories.

Suddenly the door opened and an astonished face peered in, surprised at our unexpected laughter. Our friends did not remember the advice that I had read somewhere, a paraphrase of Ecclesiastes 7:14—"in the days of adversity and affliction, forget not the good days and the pleasure of them."

Just before the memorial service the minister who was to bring the message asked me, "Do you have any special request?"

"Nothing except . . . I don't want any mantle falling on the children," I replied. "And please tell the organist to pulls the stops out. We want only really joyful music."

I felt a concern for David and Paul especially. At their ages of nineteen and seventeen, they could feel under special pressure to follow in their dad's work. Later I told them outright: "I feel Dad finished his work in Congo. There isn't anything he left for you to go finish up. But *God's* work is not finished. This same God has work in South America, India, North America, and other places as well as Congo. You must find where He wants you to work and there will be your place to serve."

As we stood in the choir room waiting to enter the memorial service Paul said, "Mother, everyone else will sing if you do."

I didn't see how I could possibly sing as we walked in and sat on the front pew. Yet when the service started, I discovered that the joyful sense of praise which we had hoped possible had become a reality. The tone of the service had been set when Mother walked down the aisle dressed in her white dress with red corsage and red hat.

Our fear that the hot August afternoon would leave only a skeleton choir was unfounded. Chairs had to be added for those who volunteered, even from other churches. We all felt it, the spirit of worship that pervaded the meeting.

Then the closing solo, "How Great Thou Art." Suddenly my mind went back to only two months before when, late one afternoon, I had completed grading some papers and walked down to the school on the Lodja Mission Station where Burleigh and I were living. Night comes quickly in the tropics. As I started home it was beginning to be dusk and the air was becoming cool as the sun dropped behind the forest surrounding the station. From the far end of the station I could hear a lawn mower puttering away; Burleigh was working at cutting the grass on the single ladies' lawn.

Over the hum of the motor I could just hear a voice singing. Then rising above the mower noise, loud and clear, I could hear, "Then sings my soul, my Saviour God to Thee, How great Thou art. . . ." The next verse was lost in the noise but the chorus rose to fill the entire station. Burleigh was singing with all his heart, completely unaware of an audience.

Two of my neighbors were visiting at the edge of a lawn as I passed. "We are just thanking God that anyone who can sing that loudly does have a good voice," one of them had said to me, laughing.

Remembering Burleigh's singing, I was aware of the words to the last verse as the soloist sang. I had never really noticed them before, but now they struck me deeply. "When Christ shall come in all His ransomed glory, And take me home, what joy shall fill my heart. Then I shall bow in humble adoration And there proclaim, 'My God how great Thou art.' " In my imagination, I could just see Burleigh singing that verse. When the last chorus came my heart was overflowing with real praise and thanksgiving.

The service was all that I had hoped it would be. I could remember other funerals which had left a terrible feeling of doom and hopelessness. But not this one. Even yet, we never begin to sing as we travel in a car that Dad's song is not among the first suggested. This says more to me about the service than even my own feelings.

Some time after the service, a friend came to call on me. "Do you know that for two years I have been fighting cancer?" she asked. I didn't. "During this time I have prayed and cried and tried my best to conquer my fear of death. Death was such a terrible threat to me. I don't know why or how, but suddenly in the service Sunday afternoon I was no longer afraid. There seemed to be something so triumphant as you and your children stood and sang and then obviously worshiped—even in such a service."

Here was the first glimmer of something working together for good.

"Will you bring Burleigh's body home?"

"Oh, no," I heard my children replying to the constant question. We all seemed to feel the same way.

"But you have no place to go to remember Burleigh," a widow commented to me one day.

"A cemetery wouldn't be any place for me to go to remember Burleigh. And I certainly hope no one will go to a cemetery to remember me," I replied. "I go where there is music and laughter to remember Burleigh—and to church on Sunday. These are the places I went with him. Besides I don't have to plan to go anywhere to remember Burleigh. Memories of him come flooding in wherever I am."

"What would you do, Virginia, if your mother-in-law insisted that you ride out to the cemetery with her every Sunday afternoon?" another friend asked.

"How long has your husband been dead?" I asked.

"Five years next month," she replied.

Imagine! Five years and still going through such a ritual. What had those weekly treks proven? I remembered my David saying, "You don't have to prove to anyone that you loved Burleigh Law." What freedom this feeling gave me. I doubted that my friend needed to prove her love and I was sure that, if there was a need for proof, it would never be fulfilled by visiting a grave.

Paul is the only member of our family who has seen Burleigh's grave. He went to Congo with a Witness-Africa team during a summer vacation. When they came to Wembo Nyama, they all went together to visit the grave. Several Congolese, seeing the team going down to the cemetery, joined them. As they stood quietly weeping, Wemb'ula, Burleigh's foreman, spoke up. "I never come down here that I don't remember how kind and patient Uwandji was with the workmen."

Then others spoke up, spontaneously sharing their memories of Burleigh. "Mother," Paul said to me, "I couldn't stand and weep when others were praising God for Dad." We found that we too couldn't weep and praise God.

While we lived in Congo, among the Batetela tribe, I

often felt that many of their funeral customs were repulsive. "This is because of their pagan rituals and practices," I said. Yet I have discovered many counterparts for their expressions here in America.

In Congo I saw the Congolese gathering up the best earthly possessions—even to new bicycles, sun helmets, pots and pans—to place on the deceased person's grave. This was their way of giving a person a "fitting burial." In a land where there is real need, it seemed such a waste for those valuables to lie there rusting and rotting away while the living family did without.

Not long after arriving in Congo we met a group of African women on the road one day. Their faces were streaked with white chalk in a grotesque design, creating a very sad, forlorn expression.

"Who are they?" I asked.

"They are the widows of the old chief who died last year," a Congolese said.

"But why all those markings?" I asked.

"Don't you know?" my informant said in a rather surprised tone. "A widow has to show her grief."

Following Burleigh's death I discovered, to my surprise, that I had this same strange desire. I felt crushed. I actually hurt at times with a sensation of physical pain that I could not quite locate. My reason for living seemed to be gone, and I wanted to show the world how I felt. For the first time in my adult life I had to force myself to take care with my grooming. A shopping trip for a necessary fall suit found me in the midst of racks of beautiful clothes, with at best, a half-hearted interest. I did finally select what has proven to be a very pretty suit, but at the time I wasn't impressed.

Not long after I bought the suit, kind friends invited me to a luncheon for a visiting dignitary—a real honor, for only a few ladies had been invited. This was the ideal time to wear my new suit.

I dressed with care that morning and just before I left my room, turned back to the mirror to check my make-up. There I suddenly saw myself as I was—dressed up. I burst into tears and fell across the bed sobbing, "I don't want to look nice. I feel sad. I want to look that way. I don't care how I look to other people!" My wail of despair and hurt and—as much as I hate to admit it—self-pity went on and on until I was drained and lay quiet.

Then, with my heart, I could see Burleigh looking down on me as if he stood at the foot of my bed. "But Virginia," he seemed to say, "you are still dressing for me. I can't tell the world that life goes on, but you can. Remember the friend who looked at you and was no longer afraid to die. Someone else may look at you and see that God's grace is sufficient even for grief, when she would not hear you tell her this."

No, I did not need to show grief. Others would see the reality of my grief easily enough. I needed to make my courage visible to someone who might need to see that.

Self-pity is the most damaging of emotions. It rises up to excuse us from our responsibilities. It gives us an excuse to get attention. It can turn its victim into a selfish, self-centered egotist who has no joy for himself and kills the joy of all others around. For me, it is the last victory won over grief.

On the other hand, you have heard of the "gay widow." I've met some of them. This is the widow who rushes out to spend her insurance money. She buys clothes she doesn't need and then lives on the road to show them off. She laughs and jokes and creates gaity which isn't joyful. She's afraid for the party to stop—then she'll have to go home. This desperate soul is fighting her battle with the wrong weapon. Grief is overcome only by joy and peace.

A grieving widow once came to me for help. Two years before, she had lost her devoted husband. Years before that she had lost her only child and at that time she had found a very real faith. The new spiritual reality had helped her through her grief, but she had also had her husband to share her burden. This time she had been alone. She had tried to pray for comfort, she had tried to believe, but nothing seemed to comfort her heart. As she talked with me I realized that the Comfort she was seeking seemed to her to be a "thing" God would give her.

"The comfort Christ promised," I told her, "isn't something like an ointment you rub on rheumatism. It is the indwelling presence of the Comforter ruling in your heart." As she began to seek Christ, she discovered that comfort came as a by-product.

Joy which overcomes grief wells up as a fruit of God's love indwelling the surrendered heart as the Holy Spirit takes control. This love heals our fears and drives away our self-pity. We worry about ourselves less and less and delight in God more and more. This is the secret of joy.

The verse which became my watchword in those days was, "Thou wilt keep him in perfect peace, whose mind is stayed on thee; because he trusteth in thee" (Isa. 26:3, KJV) . Peace which passed all understanding simply flooded my heart. Joy welled up and I could laugh and sing because God gave me a song in my heart.

Slowly the mystery of why God had permitted such tragedy began to be overshadowed by the bigger question, "Why He had given me such a sense of His presence and His joy?"

This presence of peace and joy freed me to live as normally as possible. I could actually enjoy things I had not enjoyed before. I could deliberately plan activities for myself and for my family which would make opportunities for happiness. Never once did I have to say to anyone, "Oh, I'm sorry. I can't. You see my husband has only been dead a short time."

The Congolese have a custom which had always seemed

rather unnecessary to me. "Killing the funeral" they call it.

At some time following the death of a loved one, the Congolese family sets a date to kill the time of mourning. The length of this time of grieving depends upon the importance of the deceased. We knew one big chief whose period of mourning lasted for seven years. Usually, though, it will be for eight months to a year. At the appointed time the family gathers for a feast. Chickens and goats are killed, so there is plenty of meat for everyone. Large bowls of rice are filled to overflowing. Palm wine adds to the high spirits, and village drummers beat rhythms for dancing. Every close relative must wear new clothes. The family holds a special place in the ceremonies but the entire village gathers to celebrate. Mourning is over and it is never acceptable to show grief again, for the spirit of the loved one is released to a better life.

"Just a good excuse to have a feast," had been my evaluation of this custom. Now, however, it makes better sense to me. I have seen many who would profit from it.

While discussing with a couple my travels in Europe, the husband said, "Jane and I hope to save and take such a trip one day."

"Yeah, and if I die first he'd better not go. I'll haunt him every step of the way," she added.

Surely she is just teasing, I thought. But the expression on her face and the conversation that followed gave no reason to think this true.

How different from Christ as He faced His own death! He "killed His funeral" before it began. His disciples were not to be distressed, because He was only going away to prepare a place for them—in His Father's house. And He would be coming back to take them to live with him (John 14:1-3).

Several weeks after Burleigh's death Margaret Ann crawled in bed with me one night.

"Mother," she asked, "do you know where Daddy is?"

"No, not really. All I know is that he is with Jesus. Jesus told us that He was going to make a place for those who love Him. Then He would come again and get us. I don't know just where this place is, but I do know it is a wonderful place because Jesus is there."

"You know, Mother," she said, "often at night when I'm in bed I get the funny feeling that if I could tiptoe downstairs real quiet like, I would find Dad sitting in the big chair reading. I can even see him turning his foot making his ankle pop like he did in Congo."

She paused as if remembering this and then added, "But, even more. When I'm laughing and having fun playing I feel that Daddy is standing smiling at me."

I looked down into the serene and peaceful face of my eleven-year-old Margaret Ann with joy sparkling in her eyes. As the tears in my own eyes blurred this picture, I heard deep in my heart, "You must not let yourself be distressed."

Thank God we would never have to "kill Burleigh's funeral." In reality we had never had one. We began with one pink rose to have our hearts filled with praise and thanksgiving for Burleigh.

III.

REINFORCING THE BRIDGE

"WE ARE STILL going to have a pretty home, aren't we?"

The question came from eleven-year-old Margaret Ann.

We were at Mammoth Cave, on a leisurely trip back to Florida after the second memorial service for Burleigh, in Weirton, West Virginia, his home town.

None of the children remembered being at Mammoth Cave before, but I did. The scene was quickly recreated in my mind. Burleigh and I had been in school. David was an active little boy. Paul was a baby, and Burleigh had had to carry him—we couldn't push the stroller in the cave. We didn't have much money then, but Burleigh had insisted that we stop to see the cave because he knew I wanted to. He had looked into his wallet carefully but had said nothing about the price.

Now, as we walked down the hill, I noticed a couple ahead of us. "She isn't talking to him," I thought. "She doesn't know what it is like to lose a husband. If she did she'd hold his hand. She doesn't even smile when she looks at him. Why should I lose someone I love when she still has her husband and isn't even happy with him? Why should I have to walk all alone down to the cave?"

As we entered the cave, Margaret took David's hand and Paul dropped back to walk beside me. Paul was tall like Burleigh. But Burleigh would always put his arm around me. I just fit Buleigh. My shoulder would reach just under his arm. It was so comfortable to walk with him. When we came to the slippery areas, Burleigh would always hold on to me. Paul is so sweet to hold me, I thought. He's a lot like Burleigh.

On the boat ride down the river that flows through Mammoth Cave, David sat by me. Across from us sat a radiantly happy couple. When she turned and smiled at her husband, he put his arm around her.

"Here I sit all alone"—the thought was irresistible—"no one to put his arm about me." David sensed my feeling. He reached up and put his arm around me, giving me a hug.

"But that's not the same . . . no one knows how to hug me like Burleigh did . . . no one knows how to squeeze my arm like Burleigh . . . Burleigh always knew just how to communicate his feeling . . . even an innocent squeeze could tell me a world . . . There's no one that I really belong to!"

Margaret jumped from one brother to another. She wanted a balloon. She wanted ice cream. She wanted to climb up the steepest places. She wanted to ride in the back of the boat. She talked endlessly and asked a thousand questions. As we climbed back up the hill, she came and took my hand. Looking up at me with a bright, happy expression, she asked, "We are still a family, aren't we?"

It took all the courage I could muster to answer, "Yes, we are."

Yes, we were still a family, but we didn't have a home. Everything we owned was in Congo. Burleigh and I had always worked hard to create a comfortable and attractive home, and we had enjoyed beautiful things—silver, crystal, china. But now we had only a few cheap household goods in storage. I had no hope of ever getting our things back from Congo. And I couldn't have cared less—my heart was not in selecting items for a home. Even though decorating my home had always been one of my most creative adventures, it was now only a depressing burden.

We had stopped at a crystal outlet before we got to Mammoth Cave. But that was only because I knew we would find some bargains. I bought eight each of some lovely goblets and sherbert dishes, but it wasn't at all exciting to me.

"We are still going to have a pretty home, aren't we?"

Margaret Ann's next question put my thinking into words and faced me with the choice. At that moment I realized I had a responsibility to someone beside myself. I must create the best home I could.

"Yes, we are," I said again.

After we visited Scarritt College in Nashville to arrange my entrance and housing for the fall term, we traveled on to Athens, Georgia. Friends had invited us to their lovely estate and we all felt the need of the rest. Every day of the two weeks since we had received the news of Burleigh's death had been full of activities. Meeting friends, traveling, visiting, and planning services had left us exhausted. This was our first chance to relax.

Early the first morning of our visit I went alone for a long walk through the woods. In the forest everything was quiet except the birds and the distant hum of trucks on the highway. Then I came to a stream which gurgled and sang over the rocks in its path. The sound of its music was so inviting that I sat down on a flat rock in the sunshine, pulled off my shoes and put my feet into the water. The water swirled about my feet massaging them. The warm sun on my back began to relax my body. I could feel the tension leaving me. But, suddenly, I was afraid—afraid to relax—afraid to sit quietly and be alone—afraid to think—afraid to face what I knew was ahead.

My mind rushed back over the past two weeks and I was amazed to realize just what I had faced. Who would ever have dreamed that I could have had such composure? And I really had not been forced to control myself. Somehow God had taken control. I had been placed in the hollow of His hand. As I realized this, panic subsided and my heart lifted in quiet praise; with the Apostle Paul, I had come to see that my God is able "to do exceeding abundantly above all that we ask or think. . ." (Eph. 3:20, KJV) .

But then I began to look ahead. "How am I going to move to Nashville? Who is going to pack up the few things I have stored in Tallahassee? Where did Burleigh store my dishes?"

My mind began to pile the problems up, and with them, fear started to build up in me again. "I can't even get moved . . . I'll forget something . . . how much will it cost? I don't have enough money to move . . . I'll have to pay cash . . . We'll need a car . . . I can't walk everywhere in Nashville . . . I can't carry groceries home . . . but how can I buy a car? I haven't even given the family a single thought . . . cars are terrible responsibilities . . . Burleigh always knew just what to do. He always kept our car in perfect condition."

The fear seemed to burst its bounds and flood through me. I could just see myself stranded by the road at the mercy of the world. I began to weep.

From praise and rejoicing to weeping in one moment! I felt ashamed as I realized my sudden change. "But what I have faced isn't anything like what I must face now. It isn't just me, but my children . . . David and Paul are in college . . . How will I ever pay the expenses . . . I never had to make decisions for the boys, but now I can't say, 'Ask Dad.' "

Life ahead loomed like one long, dark tunnel—I was just coming to the black entrance and would have to stumble through as best I could. Every possible decision I might face seemed to appear and add its gloom to the blackness. I found later that most of these decisions I never had to face. Certainly the horrible thought of my having to control two sons never has posed a problem. They have become my greatest source of strength and help.

"And then there's Margaret . . . Now she doesn't have a daddy. She won't ever know how to relate to men . . . a little girl learns from her daddy how to receive love from a man . . . she'll grow up abnormally . . . she'll be an old maid."

Just the thought that my little girl could possibly miss the joy of the love of a man such as I had known sent me deeper into the pit of misery.

Yet, as on and on my mind traveled, bringing up visions of problems, uncertainty, unhappiness, slowly each of these seemed to be considered and then laid aside. Someone seemed to stand there taking them into his arms, just as my kid brother used to let me stack stove wood into his outstretched arms until he couldn't see over the pile.

Slowly and quietly a thought began to move over my consciousness—"underneath are the everlasting arms."

"Everlasting arms. Ever-last-ing arms." The meaning of those words began to shine dimly as though through a deep mist. Brighter and brighter their light penetrated until they dispelled the darkness of my soul as the sun coming through a dense fog.

Everlasting means today, tomorrow, next week, next month, next year, and on, and on, and on—as long as I can possibly imagine.

"Yes!" I could feel the sure affirmation deep within my heart. "But remember, you do not need Tuesday's grace on Monday. Just walk one day at the time and trust in Me."

After a few days back in Florida, we packed to move to

Nashville. Just three weeks after our lives had been radically changed Margaret and I were at Scarritt College. David and Paul were away in other schools. I had two weeks to get situated before I began my studies for a master of arts in Christian education.

From Florida we brought with us only a few pieces of furniture and several boxes of personal belongings—really very little. Everything we needed to make a home was still in Congo. We had to get the basic things; sheets, towels, pillows, curtains, kitchen utensils, pots, pans. The list seemed endless! Where would we get the money for all these things before our small insurance policy came? I faced my first real material need.

It was utterly amazing to see how every need we had was supplied. Letters and cards of consolation poured in to us, many of them containing a small gift of money. None was big but each one bought one more item we needed. How exciting it became to get up in the morning wondering just how God was going to supply that day's needs!

I had brought only one towel and wash cloth for each of us. It soon became evident that we must have more than that. So one day "towels" was written on my shopping list. I was just going out to shop that morning, when I heard a knock at the front door. There stood the postal deliveryman with a big paper bag. I opened it to find it full of towels and washcloths, with a note telling me that this was a gift from the Martex Towel Company in appreciation of my husband's sacrificial life and death.

It was only several years later that I learned how I came to receive that gift. One of God's special Christian laymen who worked for Martex in an executive position had heard of my loss. He had felt impressed to suggest to them that they make this gift. That morning I did not know the entire story but I did know that underneath were "the everlasting arms" supplying my needs.

But even more than our needs were supplied. Margaret Ann and I went one day to the Singer Sewing Center, looking for a used machine. I had always sewed and felt lost without a machine. They didn't have a good used one at the time but were, of course, delighted to show us the new models. We looked, compared prices, even selected the nice one we would like to have someday, but went home empty-handed.

Only a few days passed when in the same mail delivery came two letters. One was from a youth group in one of the churches that had supported Burleigh and me in the Congo. They had made some money to send to us for our missionary work, but now that Burleigh was dead they wanted me to take it and buy something for our home. They were going to do another project for Congo. The other letter came from the parents of one of the missionary wives whom Burleigh had flown to rescue. "This is in appreciation for Burleigh's sacrifice to try and save our children," they wrote. "We want you to buy something you can keep to use in your home." When I added those two checks, the sum came to exactly the price of the nice sewing machine we had decided to get—some day.

We felt that we were merely standing by while God provided our every need, and many of our desires. Margaret Ann remarked one day, "I wish I had a horse."

"Be careful how you wish out loud," I teased her. "You might get one and I'll have to buy feed for it." She laughed, but she knew from the way our supplies were coming in what I meant.

Material needs are tangible and often easy to define and justify. Also, when they were supplied, anyone could see them. Yet, I found an even greater, very personal need, within myself. Suddenly left with the decisions to make for my family, I felt so terribly alone. My children were kind and helpful but I felt that, when all was said and done, I

was the one who had to make the decisions. There was no
one with whom to talk them over—no one else had to make
just these decisions. No one else began to understand them
or me as Burleigh would have. There was no one to affirm
my judgment. More than that, there was no one to affirm
me as a person.

For twenty-two years I had been awakened most morn-
ings by a big kiss. Burleigh often would get up early to see
how the workmen were doing on his building project. But
he would always return in time to slip in the bedroom and
awaken me with a kiss. He would always ask me what I
planned to do that day, because he really wanted to know.
But now, I had to wake myself, get up, and go out to face
the day with no one caring what I did. No one said to me,
"You are alive and part of my life." How could I ever live
again when no one knew that I was there?

Years ago, when I first felt a deep surge of life filling my
being, I looked around to find Burleigh looking at me. I
was a woman, and he had brought this exciting sense of being to me. Even in a crowd, or separated across a great
room, Burleigh had only to look at me with a certain gleam
in his eye and I thrilled with the sense of being a lovable,
desirable woman. Now, I had no one to affirm me. I was
simply one of the mob, lost among nine million other
widows, terribly alone. I desperately needed to feel that
someone cared for me—to have it made unmistakeably clear.
God supplied that need a few months after Burleigh's death.

I was still drawing my salary from the Methodist Board
of Missions, and the check arrived faithfully every month.
But this one month I misplaced it. It had come with other
mail, I had opened the envelope, looked at the check, and
that was the last I could remember about it. "I'm sure it is
here somewhere," I assured myself.

There was the other mail. Here was the statement from
the Board, along with some receipts for bills paid. These had

come with my check. But there was no check. Search high and low, I could not find it. I began to feel uneasy, yet I was sure I would find it the next morning when I was rested.

To my distress, the next morning I had no success. The more uneasy I became, the harder I searched until I was near panic. I needed that money that very day. To wait for the Board to replace it would be impossible. Finally, my fear that it was lost overcame me and I threw myself across the beds in tears, crying out, "Where, oh where, is my check?"

I really did not expect any answer. Yet, suddenly I had one. The impression came, "Go out and look in the trash."

"In the trash?" I looked at my watch. "That's stupid. It's already ten o'clock. I have to rush every morning to beat the trash man. Even if I did put it there, it won't be there now."

Still I could not get away from the compelling idea, "Go look in the trash!"

I dashed downstairs wearing my housecoat, and out to the side yard where the trash cans sat, near the curb. I lifted the lid—there was my garbage still waiting for the truck. Then I saw an envelope which I recognized as being from the Board. Almost fearfully I picked it up and peeked in. There was my check. My sense of awe was broken by the squeal of the brakes as the garbage truck stopped behind me. I was too overcome to ask him where he had been, or why he was so late. I still wish I knew, because never after that, that I knew about, did he come later than 8:30.

As I went back into the house, I seemed to know as I never had, "Underneath are the everlasting arms . . . arms belong to a person . . . Virginia, you are not alone! God does care for you."

In the midst of these evidences of God's care, I still had my battle with grief. A friend brought me a book with some pages marked especially for my reading which she thought would help me. But as I read it I became depressed. Here was a radiant witness of a wonderful Christian who had lost her husband and "never shed a tear." If this was the sign of spiritual depth, I didn't qualify. I shed buckets of tears. I'm sure that difference in personalities makes for difference in our expressions of grief. For myself, I never felt that my tears, poured out in the privacy of my own home, were any sign of weak faith or lack of trust. I was hurt and lonely. Life just didn't offer the happiness and contentment I had known. I seemed to build up emotions and then some small incident would pull the trigger. Tears would flow.

Yet to be perfectly honest, I had to admit that tears did not really help. I rushed home one day on the verge of tears. No one was there so I gave loud, vocal vent to all the grief I felt. My sobs filled the house. The more I cried, the more I felt like crying. For more than two hours I cried. Then I realized that I felt worse than when I started. Crying had not done any good.

Still crying, I got up, straightened my hair, washed, and made up my face—then went out for a walk. Since crying was not the answer, I must find some other way to handle my grief.

As I walked I prayed—not really a verbalized prayer in my mind but an upward look of my heart saying, "Father, surely You have some other way through this dark tunnel." Slowly and quietly peace filled me. I had learned a hard lesson. The comfort God had promised had to be received. He wasn't going to force it upon me. I had to open my broken heart to let the comfort enter.

This incident did not end my tears, but I never let grief take control of me again. Instead I cried out to God, not trying to pretend or to hide my feelings of hurt, frustration, loneliness but rather expressing them openly and honestly. John tells us that Jesus "did not need anyone to tell him what people were like: he understood human nature" (John 2:25, Phillips) . I believed this. I knew that God under-

stood and I felt He suffered with me. He was hurt that one
of His children was going through such agony. Yet again and
again I was forced to realize that if I had not had so much in
my marriage my loss would have been less. I often discovered
that my prayers which had begun in despair ended in
praise—"Thank you, Father, for a husband who was so
wonderful that I am hurt to lose him."

Like others, I was tempted to feel that my loss was the
greatest. No one could ever have loved so deeply, nor suffered so greatly as I was suffering.

As I listened to the trials of a widow left with a big
business to settle, I found myself reacting; "But what if you
were like me without anything to sell?"

"My great big house is so lonely."

"What if you didn't even have a house?"

"My children are all grown and gone."

"What if you had a little girl to raise without her daddy?"

"It is costing so much to educate my son."

"What if you had two sons in college and no financial
resources?"

It really didn't matter what anyone suffered in grief, I
felt that I had suffered more than they.

Once I heard a widow say, "If only I could understand.
Why should I lose John when we were so in love? My
neighbors who don't care about their husbands still have
them. . . . We were serving God. We were doing everything
we could for Him. But now my whole life has been wrecked.
I don't see the fairness in it."

As she shared her heartbreak with me I could readily
identify. Wasn't the same true of Burleigh and me? Weren't
we serving God? Then I thought of a wonderful single lady
whom I had known on the mission field. She had offered
God all that I had, and more. She had served alone on a
missionary field where marriage prospects were nil. "What
did you ever do to deserve such a wonderful missionary

husband?" I was forced to ask myself. Then I knew that when I could answer that question I might have the right to ask the other questions.

Only when one has been so deeply wounded in grief can he fully understand the actual pain that goes with it. I felt as if my whole chest were one great big open wound, sensitive and bleeding. In the days immediately following the loss, everything reminded me of Burleigh. I had no recent memories that did not involve him. I had lived so close to him, in both work and play, that he was just always there. Now in my grief, he came again and again to mind.

My situation was made more difficult by the length of time required to learn the details surrounding Burleigh's death. First came the phone call from the board of missions. Late that afternoon came a telegram from the U.S. State Department making official the news. The next morning came a cablegram simply saying, "Burleigh buried at Wembo Nyama." Then almost a week passed with no news. The next word came from a friend who sent me a letter from her husband in Congo. He had written that Burleigh had flown over to Wembo Nyama. Her letter was written two days later and she had heard no more news. Another week of agonizing, unanswered questions passed while floods of letters of condolence arrived—almost as if I were being comforted for a loss I had not yet had.

Then one day I lifted out my mail from the mailbox. "Oh, no! It can't be! It just can't be!"

But it was! Here was a blue airmail lettergram in my hand—a letter from Burleigh! On Sunday evening, before his death on Tuesday, he had written me a lovely long letter in his scrawling, often illegible handwriting. He just couldn't be dead! Here he was telling about flying, about Barbara Norris going on vacation, about bringing some supplies up to Wembo Nyama where he almost stayed overnight since "my big reason for coming home wasn't here." He told how he had slept late, how he and Joe had gone down to get the mail, and since they didn't have the key, he had picked the lock. He said my letter from Brussels was there and how sweet of me to write, even on my trip home. There had also been a long letter from Paul telling Burleigh how much he meant to him. He talked of how wonderful it was to be the father of teenage sons who said "Thank you."

Then there was a long paragraph written as he looked about our living room describing how everything he saw reminded him of me; the carved praying hands that we had bought in Germany, the silver cup David got for being the outstanding athlete of the year in Brussels and our pride at being the parents of such a boy, the fine China he gave me on Mother's Day, the brass plate bought in Athens. He reminded me of our moonlight cruise on the Aegean Sea. After rambling on and on about all the love and life we had shared, he ended, "Have a good time. Enjoy yourself, but do hurry home when September 6th comes. I don't really live when you're not here. I love you more than I could ever love anyone for I love you as God's special gift to me."

"I don't really live when you're not here." That's it! I can't live without Burleigh, I thought. *He can't be dead. I have a letter from him.*

Then came my first real information in a letter written by a heartbroken missionary. It showed all the grief but some parts simply did not make sense. With all the letters that came, none seemed really to answer my questions. Those answers were just too painful for those who knew them to tell. It was not until three months later, when the missionary men who were held hostages by the rebels were finally released, that one of my friends in the group sat down and bravely answered what questions he could.

During those days a small package came. When I opened it something fell out. I looked down and there at my feet on the rug lay Burleigh's wedding ring. Someone had slipped it off of his finger to send to me. At first I simply stared at it. Then I closed my eyes. I couldn't stand to look. It seemed that some evil spirit was laughing at me. "See! He sent you back his ring. He isn't yours any more!"

There is something healthy about a funeral. It is a forceful reminder that one really has laid away his loved one. I did not have that memory to force me to face reality. I did have the ring, a fact which made me admit its owner was absent but was not forceful enough to be therapeutic.

Burleigh's New Testament was also in the package. This small Bible he had always carried in his shirt pocket. Now I opened it and saw that the corners were blood-stained. Burleigh really had been wounded. He had bled.

Finally, there were some slides and a tape recording of the funeral. There were pictures of the Congolese carrying a crude homemade casket on their shoulders with a homemade spray of native flowers lying on top. But worst of all, Wemb'ula, Burleigh's foreman, was wearing one of Burleigh's suits. The tape, all in Otetela, told of the grief of those people. Above the service I could hear the weeping. Hearing the tape brought the conviction, "Burleigh really has been buried. He has a grave."

Although I lived in Nashville, I still did not consider it "home." This was just temporary. I did have a home in Congo. Almost everyday I needed something that I didn't have, but I had that article in Congo.

Then one day an express truck delivered a large trunk. When I opened it, I found in its musty, mildewed interior every earthly possession my friends could possibly salvage from our looted home. Now every memory I had of a lovely Congolese home was reduced to one musty trunk. I really did not have a home. It, too, was gone—buried in the same soil as was Burleigh.

This can't be true, I thought. *But it has to be . . . I couldn't have lost more . . . I can't stand such pain . . . The*

agony is going to stifle the very life out of me . . . Father,
take away this pain.

I now realize that what I really wanted was for God to
anesthetize my emotions. I didn't want to feel grief. I wanted
Him to deaden my memory, to take away my hurt and
frustration. Maybe if I could just pray enough, and somehow
find faith enough to believe, this would happen.

I tried to be anesthetized for several weeks and yet I had
to admit that I saw no great improvement. Then one day I
sat quietly thinking about my need. What was I really wanting? Did I really want to be made so insensitive to my own
hurt and loss? What would that do to my ability to feel for
other people in grief?

I remembered an incident that occurred on our first term
at Wembo Nyama. Burleigh was busy trying to transport tons
of heavy machinery up from Lusambo, where the river
barges docked, to our station at Wembo Nyama. Never had
such machines come to that part of Congo. The well-driller
and sawmill, stripped of every piece that could possibly be
removed, still weighed more than five tons. Added to this
was the weight of the big Brockway truck—making a total of
at least eight tons.

Between Wembo Nyama and Lusambo there were many
bridges. Some crossed small streams but many spanned deep,
swirling streams. All of the bridges were constructed from
the most fragile materials. Poles and logs had been cut and
sawed from the forest trees and joined together by a native
vine. Then across the top more poles formed the bed of the
bridge. Sometimes a few boards on the very top formed a
track for the wheels, but often there was nothing. At most
of them stood a sign warning "3 T."—three tons was the
tested weight capacity. Occasionally there was a "5 T." But
nowhere was there an "8 T." bridge.

Below in the swirling streams snakes hid among logs and
rocks. In some there were even crocodiles waiting for their

supper. The very possibility that Burleigh might end up falling into one of these streams as he drove the heavily loaded truck across such a bridge filled me with fear. I could not help but let him know of my distress. But he didn't seem to understand why I should be so upset.

"What are you going to do about such weight on those bridges?" I asked.

He paused, as if in deep thought. Then, looking down at me and in a confident voice, he said, "There isn't anything I can do to lighten the load. I'll just have to reinforce the bridge." And that's what he did. He cut extra poles and placed them underneath each bridge just long enough for the load to pass over. More than 60 tons of heavy machinery made it safely up to Batetela Land.

As I reflected on this, I understood the message. There really wasn't anything God could do to lighten my load. In any heartbreak such as I was experiencing there is just so much hurt, so much pain, so much loneliness. These are a part of human emotions and God does not deaden or take them away. He does not lighten the load. But He does reinforce the bridge.

The everlasting arms underneath are there to reinforce the bridge. No longer would I blame or accuse myself when I did not feel brave. When I was aware of my own human emotions, looking up I'd say, "Father, I need the reinforcements." Each time they were given; I could feel the load going over while He supported me with His everlasting arms.

IV.

~~

TAKE CARE

In the early days of my grief nothing seemed to make sense. A certain amount of disorientation was the natural result of coming home from Congo. Even on a regular furlough there had always been months of adjustment. But the shocking grief, moving to a strange town, unexpectedly entering college again—everything seemed to compound my problem. The adjustment seemed at times impossible.

One of my professors called me in one day. "Virginia, I'm afraid you are expecting more of yourself than anyone has any right to expect," she said.

Her genuine interest in me and her wisdom gained through years of teaching made her sensitive to the strain that I faced daily. "Make a list of everything you can start doing to humor yourself," she advised me.

"Like what?" I asked.

"I don't know. That is your list. What don't you do just for yourself that you really can do? You see, Virginia, you are a person with a great deal of drive and energy. For years you have had Burleigh to say to you, 'Come on. Leave that. It can wait.' Now you don't have him. If you don't start stopping yourself to do relaxing activities, you'll break down your strong body and suddenly collapse one day."

She was a woman I admired, and I especially appreciated the interest and advice from someone who had accomplished so much in life. I went home and made my list.

"Get my hair set at the beauty parlor each week." I had been doing it at home and dusting while it dried. Just leaving my home and sitting under a dryer was relaxing. I didn't take any books, either. I looked at the magazines there. I didn't learn much from them but, interestingly, I found that merely reading something so far removed from my own life was a change of pace.

"Eat Sunday dinner at Scarritt." This was another treat Margaret Ann and I could afford. They always had lovely meals there, served with style. But more important, we sat with different students each week and came to know many of them well. It gave us and them a feeling of family fellowship.

The list grew as I pondered. I was surprised at just how many things I really could do to help relieve the tension and stress of my everyday life.

How grateful I have been for the interest and advice of that professor. If she had been a lazy, unambitious woman who had never accomplished anything herself, I might have been tempted to disregard her advice. But she was not. My only regret was that I had not realized sooner how, in my desire to be brave, I had exposed myself to more real pain than was necessary.

I was much like my son David when he was approaching his ninth birthday in Congo. For this happy occasion, we had promised him a long weekend at a small lake some distance from our mission station. Our mission owned a small camp cottage there and that was all there was. But we could swim, and more important for David, there was good hunting. David was really anticipating the treat of going out with his dad and handling his big guns.

We made our trip to the lake and, sure enough, Burleigh took David with him early the next morning and to walk around the lake—a good ten-mile trip. Near noon they came dragging in, with the Congolese carrying a big antelope which Burleigh had killed and a small one that David had hit. I noticed that David was limping slightly, but I didn't think this strange after such a walk until I saw that the right hip of his jeans was wet.

"What's wrong with your jeans?" I asked.

"Oh, nothing," he said, looking away.

Something about his answer, and the look in his eyes, made me wonder. "Come here. Let me see," I said.

He came rather reluctantly. I looked in and saw that his underpants were wet with a yellow fluid. Then, I looked at his hip. There was a big red abscess which had swollen, burst, and was draining. A shot he had taken weeks before had become abscessed.

David had known this for several days. But, not one word had he said for he was afraid it might cancel our trip or his hunt. If only he had admitted it we could have had it lanced and given him antibiotics. By the time for our trip, he would have been nearly healed. His saying, "I'm not hurting," had not taken away his pain.

My attempts to say, "I'm not suffering in grief," although I did not realize them to be such, were not removing the suffering this had brought to me. It began to show up in my body. I began to suffer from headaches, neck cricks, tight shoulder muscles, and arthritic-like joints.

One afternoon while I was practice teaching, I felt a sharp pain in my chest. I finished out the day, went home, took some antacid pills, and rested. I felt some better until late bedtime and then I felt worse. When I realized just how late it was, I really did feel pain. I did the usual arguing with myself. I was sure it wasn't my heart, but scared to death it might be. How foolish I was to suffer the rest of the night in such painful fear, but I did. Only my pride in my bravery kept me from calling my kindly doctor.

Early the next morning I did call and met the doctor at a nearby hospital. He examined me and ordered me admitted. I was to stay in bed except for going in a wheel chair to the toilet. For two days I had a "No Visitors" sign on my door. He didn't give a diagnosis but I got the impression that it might be my heart.

For a whole week I rested there in the hospital. All kinds of tests were made. Finally, my day of dismissal came. My doctor came in and stood by my bed. "We have not found anything really organically wrong," he said. "There is some irritation in your duodenum. It isn't anything serious that a couple weeks of bland diet won't cure. This is what I thought when I admitted you. But I felt you needed a week of absolute rest and you've had that."

As I went home, I could not believe how much better I felt. I had not had the slightest idea of how much strain my nerves and muscles were suffering. I knew then without a doubt that if I did not find some means to release my grief, I would finally break.

"How happy are those who know what sorrow means, for they will be given courage and comfort."* I don't feel that everyone has to get into the hospital to realize how sorrow can affect even our bodies but I do think everyone must realize what his own sorrow is doing to him before he can be comforted. Some find this out much earlier that I did, but some never find it.

We often seem to have a strange idea of what is demanded of a person suffering grief. I have already told of my distress when someone shared with me a book telling how one widow

* Matt. 5:4 Phillips.

lost her husband and "never shed a tear." I'm certain this lady was brave and her witness has blessed many people, but I could not relate to it. I simply could not face my loss without tears. I tried never to cry in public. Several times I quietly slipped out when I felt I couldn't control the tears.

On the other hand, I know another person who simply could not control her tears. They flowed too easily and quickly, yet they had a refreshing effect on her and others.

In contrast, I had known, in my earlier life, an elderly lady who for years had carried dainty, white, lace-trimmed hankies. At the most inappropriate time, she would take one out and dab her eyes ever so gently. Everyone would stop what they were doing and turn very solicitously to see what caused her tears. Without further details from me, you can see what happened next. With half a tear in each eye she could command stage center.

Despite my genuine attempt to be brave, I had a shocking revelation one day. I had found that tears were filling my eyes and overflowing down my cheeks. I hastily wiped them and no one seemed to pay the least attention. I was insulted. Here I was suffering such agony and no one cared. Then, when all alone, I found a persistent question demanding an answer. "Why did it matter to you whether anyone noticed or not?"

I remembered the little old lady with her white hankie. "Is it possible that tears are a way to gain the attention you have lost?" Self-pity is such a subtle, deceitful enemy because it so often appears to be working against grief when it actually is grief's strongest ally.

In painful thought I had to look at myself. I could see that much too often my tears were really "poor me" being expressed in a socially acceptable way. I would never have sat down to tell anyone how terrible was my plight. I was too brave for that; but a few tears could accomplish the same thing.

As I faced myself in remembering my white lace hankie friend, I seemed to hear, "Virginia, you must choose either self-pity or spiritual victory. You can't have both. You can go through life fluttering your little white hankie just often enough to ruin everyone else's fun, or you can give up self-pity and let God's grace give you a joyful, radiant life. It is as simple as that."

There is a very thin line between self-pity, which must go, and self-consideration, which must stay. Only the person in grief can decide for himself where this line is.

There was too much "God helps those who help themselves" in my philosophy for this to be an easy lesson. Yet, there were too many times when I realized I couldn't help myself.

It was months later that I really understood what I had heard the day of Burleigh's death. "You have to surrender," now made sense. Or, maybe I realized that, although I had surrendered then, I had resumed fighting. I was like the old man with a heavy load on his back who was offered a ride. Sitting in the back of the wagon riding along he kept this burden still strapped to his back.

"Why don't you put down your load?" he was asked.

"Oh, you're so kind to carry me that I don't want to give you my burden, too."

I felt that God was carrying me but I was still handling my burden. "Maybe I don't know what comfort really is," I said. "If I did, I might really find it."

"How happy are those who know what sorrow means, for they will be given courage and comfort." For me to know what sorrow means, I had to experience the real pain of sorrow. Yet I had also to see what it did to me, the tensions and strain it brought, the self-pity it created. And I had to realize that sorrow was stronger than I, while, on the other hand, the opposite of sorrow—peace and joy—are not qualities we can strain and labor to produce, but they are qualities which beautifully flow into our hearts as the gift of God.

In a public square near the apartment in Belgium we lived in several years ago, there was a large fountain. Somehow it had stopped flowing. Soon the water around it became a stagnant pool. Dark and grimy it stood. Then one day the fountain started gushing forth. Gallons of clear, pure water rolled down and overflowed from the pool into its drains. Slowly the scum broke up from the pool's surface and floated away. The churning water rinsed the pool itself and even the muddy bottom became clear. All the dirt and grime was cleansed away by the flowing water.

Comfort was not a thing I could secure like an ointment. It was not a reward for my efforts or an accomplishment I achieved. God's comfort was His presence coming to fill my very being and drive away my sorrow. The greatest lesson I had to learn about sorrow was that it was not something Virginia could ever handle herself.

The ultimate healing of all our sorrows will come when "the Lamb . . . shall lead them unto living fountains of waters; and God shall wipe away all tears from their eyes" (Rev. 7:17, KJV).

In many tall vaulted cathedrals throughout Europe are beautiful stained glass windows made from small pieces of vari-colored glass worked into a most intricate design of a rose. A legend often told us as we stood admiring such beauty said that the first colored glass windows were large sheets of glass. The first cathedral to be so decorated had many windows of different colors and hues. No two windows were the same. The villagers were so proud of their windows that they bragged far and wide about them. People came great distances to see and admire the beautiful colors of these large windows.

Then one night a terrible storm raged through the village. The next morning the villagers came out to find every window had been blown out and lay broken in great big jagged pieces on the floor. Their hearts were broken. They couldn't bear to go look at this destruction. Finally one brave soul went down to the cathedral.

There he found the master craftsman sitting on the floor carefully breaking those big jagged pieces of glass into small, tiny pieces.

"He's lost his mind," the man said. "What does he mean? Doesn't he know that it is broken enough. What possible good could come from breaking it more?"

Little did he dream what was in the mind and heart of that master craftsman. From those tiny broken pieces he created the first Rose Window.

I wondered what kind of a rose window God was planning to make out my broken life.

V.

✒

WHERE WAS GOD?

"Never ask 'Why?' " is good advice, but I know of no way that a person can completely avoid that question. At times I could, and yet again I couldn't. Nor could some of my missionary friends. One confided in me his own doubts. He had represented our Batetela area at a special meeting to study the future of the literacy work in Congo.

For an effective program they needed a press—but who would keep it going with Burleigh gone? They needed distribution—Burleigh had repaired the cars. They needed supplies—Burleigh had flown those in when necessary. Everywhere they turned, they faced the loss of Burleigh. Didn't God realize how much depended on Burleigh in our mission work?

Yet I knew that God had repeatedly instructed me not to ask "Why?" For the most part I avoided the question as much as possible. I prayed that I could hold on by faith as I walked through the dark tunnel. I knew that if I could ever just get down the road far enough to look back and see the pattern, then maybe I could understand why. Yet, I realized that when I got that far along the answer to my question wouldn't really be important. I can't imagine that when I meet Burleigh again we will even discuss the "why." We'll have more than that to say.

At times, though, I had to admit that by avoiding the question, I had allowed it to take a more subtle form—"Where was God when this happened?"

First of all, this question threatened my conviction that God had guided Burleigh's life. When I first met him—back in college twenty-three years before—it was his certainty that he knew what God wanted him to do with his life that most impressed me. It was our mutual interest in serving God that had drawn Burleigh and me toward each other.

As we dated on the campus of Asbury College in Kentucky, our dreams were built around Burleigh's dedication to be a missionary. This dedication had not come easily. Only after months of resisting, when he was convinced this was God's revelation, had he made the surrender of his own will to God's will and found this true dedication.

We often strolled around the semicircle on the front campus hand in hand, sharing and building together our dreams. When time came to say goodnight, we would stop about halfway around at a special spot. From there we could look up through the trees and see the large neon cross lighted on top of the tall smokestack. Still holding hands we would sing softly:

> Follow, I will follow Thee, my Lord
> Follow, every passing day.
> Our tomorrows are all known to Thee.
> Thou wilt lead us all the way.

Burleigh would squeeze my hand, kiss me goodnight and then walk with me to the dorm. As we walked, my heart would be filled with joy. Yes, with joy but with more than joy. I felt lifted up with excitement and challenge that I was a part of some great plan which God had for this young man, and I had no fear. My confidence was based on God and His plan—but more than that—on His ability to lead us into that plan.

Now looking back, I still believed that God had guided. Burleigh's dream of being a missionary had been gloriously fulfilled. More wonderful still, God had let me be a part of making that dream come true. I could not believe that Burleigh would ever have been as happy doing anything as he was serving on the mission field. And, deep within my heart, I believed that my happiness to be there with him, despite hard and difficult days, was a big factor in his joy. Yes, I had to believe that it was God who had led us to the mission field.

"But was that the end of God's guidance? Did He really continue to lead you?" I asked myself. "Yes, I honestly believe He did," I could answer.

After seven years at Wembo Nyama, the oldest and largest Methodist Mission Station in Central Congo, Burleigh had developed a very active group of African laymen who were eager to share their Christian witness. At this time we were experiencing the greatest mass movement in new converts that our church had known. Most of this was concentrated in the northern part of our Lodja District. We took a group of the workmen and went to share in a revival at a remote village.

The weekend was full of excitement and challenge as we saw people arriving, carrying their suitcases wrapped in blankets on their heads. Many of them had walked for more than fifty miles. Most of them had come because they had heard reports of real transformations in the hearts of people.

Some came to hear, for the first time, the message of God's love revealed in Christ. So it was with a group of the

Esongomena clan. For more than forty years the church had been trying to slowly reach into their area. Still they had resisted—just as they resisted every new idea of change the white man had brought.

The Belgian colonial officials had long before given up trying to force them to accept more modern ways to farm, build roads, or bring sanitation. Later, when I visited their village, I saw what their resistance had really meant.

Late one afternoon Burleigh and I walked down through an Esongomena village visiting with the people. It was time for their one big meal of the day. The people were gathered in the back yard near the kitchen. We paused from house to house for a few moments to chat.

As Burleigh talked with the men about hunting, I was listening and looking around. Suddenly it dawned on me what I was actually seeing. The food, all locally grown, was being cooked in a large clay pot made in their village. The stove was three black round ant hills resembling bowling balls. On these sat the pot. They served the food with a carved wooden spoon, placing it on a clean banana leaf. This leaf was spread on a large, woven mat. Around this the men sat on the ground, ate with their fingers, and drank water from a gourd. There was not a single implement of Western culture in the entire operation. Then I really understood how complete had been their rejection of the white man.

When a runner came from this clan bringing word that they were coming to the revival, real excitement went through the village. This was their first evidence of any interest in the Christian message.

When they arrived, their unique facial markings made them easily identified. Custom dictates that at about eight years of age a child's face is cut in what they consider an attractive cicatrice design. Tiny pieces of crude rubber are placed in these cuts, so that they heal over leaving a permanent hobnail effect. They wear their hair long and pulled back in a roll along the back of the head. They file their teeth to sharp points.

As the Esongomenas sat listening intently to their first message of God's love, I wondered what it must be like to hear it for the first time. How different my life would have been had I lived among them! Then, at the close of the service, one of these men knelt at the altar for prayer. Rising from his knees he confessed to cannibalism, saying, "I was in darkness and did not know."

This confession deeply moved both Burleigh and me. We discussed it again and again. The need for a missionary to live and work among this and other clans in the Lomela area distressed Burleigh. "I believe God is calling us to go up and work among them," he said one day.

"Oh, Burleigh. I don't think He is. That wasn't what I had in mind when I was praying for them," came my quick reply. I really couldn't see it. I had many reasons why I disagreed, but the main reason I was ashamed to voice. We had only been back from furlough a little over a year. The house we occupied had needed drastic repairs that had taken all that time to finish. Not only our time, but our paint from America had been put in that house. I had cut my new drapery materials to fit the windows and cover the chairs. The house had finally been transformed into "home." Leaving this pleasant home to move to a vacant plot of forest where there wasn't anything seemed to be too much of a sacrifice to consider.

Besides my deep personal feeling, I felt it was unfair to our five-year-old, Margaret Ann. She would be away from all English-speaking playmates. She would also be giving up her home to move into a crude shelter. More seriously, she would be 300 miles from a missionary doctor. Suppose she became ill with cerebral malaria; we could not possibly get medical help in time. I could imagine all kinds of terrible emergencies arising with us isolated in the forest.

Then, too, Burleigh had worked for eight years on the Lambuth Memorial Hospital. He had slaved at moving the heavy machines in over those impossible roads between Wembo Nyama and Lusambo. He had installed them, then made the bricks and cut the lumber. Long, hard, unrewarding days of sweat and blood had gone into that hospital. Now it stood more than half completed. I wanted him to be there when it was finished—to get in on the cheering. (Never did I dream that his part in building that hospital would be heralded to the world.)

Both of us were so busy and involved carrying heavy loads of missionary tasks that I could not imagine it being even wise to consider leaving Wembo Nyama for another station. Each time it came up, I gave my resistance—stronger and stronger. I began to realize that it was distressing Burleigh. He felt God was calling him to Lomela and I wasn't hearing this same call. Looking back, I can now realize that I had begun to be uneasy with my objections, but not uneasy enough to really look at them.

We were to have Dr. E. Stanley Jones out to Wembo Nyama for a Conference-wide Ashram. I was busy preparing for it, excited over the guests we would entertain. Just as the big job was completed, I received an urgent request. One of our missionary ladies was ill and had asked to come over as a guest in my home. Would I kindly agree to take her? Of course I would! Yet this meant that I would not be free to attend the Ashram as I had planned. I was left sitting quietly at home nursing my friend while I listened to the joyful singing and talking coming from the Ashram across the station. There was plenty of time to think and to pray— and I found myself looking at my objections to going to Lomela.

As I meditated I realized for the first time how distressed Burleigh really was. He loved me deeply. It pained him even to consider a change in our lives which I did not approve.

And he was puzzled. I had accepted coming to Congo with enthusiasm. Yet, as he felt God leading us to Lomela, I was not only unenthusiastic, I was obviously against the idea. Slowly the Spirit began to help me honestly see my objec-- tions. Then I realized, deep in my heart, "God is calling Burleigh."

When once I had come to see this clearly, I could begin to pray for a willing heart.

I was right. Burleigh had been torn by two loyalties. He could not believe that God was leading him to go and was not at the same time dealing with me. This concern was on his mind during the Ashram. In a time of prayer he had finally accepted this sense of call to be from God. In a painful moment of surrender he had said, "Yes, Lord, I'll go even if Virginia never agrees with my call." (Burleigh knew that there was no question of my not going with him if he decided to go. It was, rather, a question of my happiness which distressed him.)

That afternoon he stood at the "Service of the Overflowing Heart" and gave a witness that no one hearing it really understood. Dr. Jones related it in his book *The Power of Surrender,* but without knowing all that Burleigh had meant when he said, "I love my wife too much. I've been listening to her instead of to God." What a joy for both of us when finally the Ashram was over and we could share what had happened to us both.

We moved to Lomela and it was just as difficult as I had imagined in my worst moments. Our living conditions were crude beyond imagination. We were the only missionaries in the area. We had a dog get rabies and had no medical advice to cope with it. The light motor went dead while Burleigh was away on business, and I was alone for ten long dark nights. But what a challenging experience! In retrospect I had to admit, "If God would offer me two years of my life to relive, I'd take those two." Our marriage came into an even deeper level of communication. More than ever I felt, "Here is a man whom God truly guides." Burleigh realized anew what my enthusiasm and cooperation meant to him.

Now as I looked back on our life of service together, I knew these two years could be considered one of the high spots. I also knew that if God had listened to me I would never have gone to Lomela. Slowly the thought stirred in me—can it be that in the hardest experiences of life we find our deepest rewards?

Perhaps this realization was to be the first ray of light in the tunnel of my shattered life. If I could only believe and trust until the pattern was revealed. I could believe that God had guided us to Congo. I could believe that He had guided us during our life there, but that still did not answer my real question, "Where was God when this happened?"

True, I needed to find a faith that could patiently wait and trust. "But how can I really trust a God who, it seems to me, had let Burleigh down?" Never would I have been honest enough to voice this doubt to anyone, but that did not stop me from doubting. My own questioning placed me in a terrible dilemma. "Was God helpless? Maybe He couldn't have done anything about it. But surely He could have at least fogged in the airstrip. In dry season that would not take a miracle. If God closed the sky for the Kole missionaries, why not for Burleigh?"

This agonizing thought grew out of an experience Burleigh had had one day flying from Katubwe to Lodja. Very suddenly the sky grew dark with dangerous thunder clouds. Banking about to look at the sky, Burleigh lost his direction. When he spotted one blue opening in the entire horizon, he flew toward it and kept flying through it. With relief he saw an air strip below. As he flew low, he saw the name "Kole" marked in white stones. He landed.

Hardly had he cut his engine when a lady rushed up.

With tears in her eyes she told how, isolated there with no transportation and a desperately ill missionary, they had prayed for help. Burleigh was their answer. Burleigh immediately flew back out of Kole to Wembo Nyama and brought back Dr. Hughlett. What an experience for Burleigh! He had told this story again and again. The God he served was able to close the sky to answer His child's prayer.

"Do you believe that, Virginia?" I had to answer this painful question and I could not fool myself. "Yes, I believe it."

The Creator is greater than His creation. It wouldn't really take a miracle. It would be so easy for just the natural processes of nature to work. "So, if God could so easily have prevented Burleigh's landing at Wembo Nyama and didn't, why didn't He?"

How I wished that I knew, but I finally had to admit, "I don't know."

Even with that question unanswered, I still could not disregard what I had believed through the years—God was guiding us!

But more than that, I had believed that He was moving before us, making possible our fulfilling His will and protecting us as we served.

When we were young, just ready to make our final preparation for missionary service, we had faced a real need for experience but no opportunity to get it. Then, from out of the blue, Burleigh had been offered a job as an instructor in mechanics, a custom-made job for his need. So miraculous did this seem that we had taken it as a positive affirmation that going to Congo was God's will. Again and again, in trying and difficult days, we had recalled this affirmation and drawn new courage from it. So, I believed that not only did God have a will for Burleigh but that He could make possible its fulfillment. I had to believe that this same God had a will for Burleigh—yes, even on August 4th, 1964.

If this really had been true, then, "Where was God that fateful day? Was it possible He had been there trying to protect Burleigh but couldn't reach him?"

When I reached this point in my dilemma, I heard an interesting story. A certain girl was traveling one day by train. The train had stopped at a station to discharge passengers. As she was waiting for the train to pull out again, she suddenly felt strongly impressed to leave the train. Looking around she could see no reason to leave. Yet, even more definite and strong was the impression, "Get out!"—an impression she recognized as being from God.

Without further delay she rushed down the car leaving her bags and barely reached the platform before the train began to move. She was still in the terminal trying to decide what to do when she heard the news. Her train had just reached its full speed when it had hit a closed switch on the edge of town and was wrecked. When the full story was known, she knew that the very car in which she was. riding had been demolished. Most of its passengers were dead.

"How unfair," I said, feeling terrible rebellion against a God who would only tell one girl to get off a train doomed to wreck. When my rebellion had spent itself, I heard quiet questions being raised. "How do you know how many people God tried to reach who just didn't hear? How do you know how hard God might have cried to the switchman who had one drink too many to think clearly? Or, how loudly He could have called to the engineer who forgot to watch his signals because, perhaps, he was too busy preparing an alibi for his wife to explain the night before. How do you know?"

I had to admit that I didn't know all that went into that experience. Really, all I did know was that one girl, sensitive to God's voice, and schooled in obedience, had heard, acted, and been spared.

I had made some progress. I could affirm in honesty that I did believe God had a plan for Burleigh on that fateful

August 4th. I had to admit that, in past events, Burleigh had needed to hear God's voice in order to be rescued from danger, just as had the girl on the train. How much suffering and disaster comes upon us because we simply do not and will not heed God's efforts to communicate with us! But most painful for me was the question, "Was Burleigh not listening?"

Then how beautifully it dawned upon me that Burleigh was listening and that he had left us a witness that he was. The missionaries had told me that one of them asked, as he found Burleigh lying wounded by the plane, "Didn't you see our signal not to land?"

Burleigh answered, "Yes, I saw it and I tried three times to fly away but I couldn't go to safety and do nothing to rescue you."

In my imagination I could easily reenact that scene. Burleigh saw the signal down below and turned to fly back to Lodja. Then he felt impressed to fly back into danger so he turned toward Wembo Nyama. Hardly was he headed for danger than he realized what he was doing. How silly to be deliberately flying into danger! A second time he banked around to get his direction for Lodja. Another impression that he should rescue his fellow missionaries. A longer deliberation this time, but again he turned for Wembo Nyama and danger. Now he faced what might actually happen. His own desire for safety and self-preservation welled up. He simply didn't have such courage and for the third time he turned toward home and safety. But, again, he felt uneasy. The impression was unmistakable. Without further hesitation he turned and headed for Wembo Nyama and death. This is, of course, only my imaginary account, but it is true to the Burleigh I knew.

I do know that three times he tried to fly away. Three times he turned back. I cannot believe that facing such a decision Burleigh failed to listen and hear God speak.

Now I can believe that God was present. I can believe
Burleigh was listening. "But surely you don't believe God
had anything to do with Burleigh's death?" friends asked
me in utter shock. "Haven't you read about the perfect will,
the permissive will, and the ultimate will of God?"

Yes, I had read about these. But to me the concept seemed
to put God on a mop-up crew. God appeared to be standing
by helplessly, until the paint was spilled, and then He'd start
working it together for good.

Already, though, I could begin to see that God was working the aftermath for good for Burleigh. Reports had
reached me that our Congolese friends had realized the real
nature of the communist-backed rebel movement when the
rebels had killed Burleigh.

But, even more beautiful, at Easter I received a precious
letter from a Congolese. "This has been a very special Easter
to all of us," he wrote. "Until this year we believed that
Jesus forgave the enemies who killed Him, because the missionaries told us that He did. Now we believe because
Uwandji showed us that He did." He was referring to Burleigh's dying word, "Don't blame him [meaning the rebel
soldier]. He didn't understand me."

While reading the account of Jesus in the Garden of
Gethsemane, my son Paul said, "Mother, did you realize
that Jesus tried three times to avoid Calvary? Three times
He prayed and each time He knew He'd have to go." He
paused a moment and added, "Dad tried three times to
stay away from Wembo, didn't he?"

Maybe I found the answer to my question, "Where was
God when Burleigh went to Wembo?" in the answer a minister gave to another person with such a question: "The
same place He was when His own Son went to Calvary."

Just beginning to see some good coming out of my
tragedy comforted my heart beyond measure. But I had to
be honest. A God who could only work after the tragedy had

happened was only adequate for Burleigh for whom tragedy could not strike again. It was not enough for me—still facing decisions and dangers.

Such a complicated theological question! Men far smarter than I have wrestled with it for centuries. Could I ever really understand or would I have to blindly believe? Was I doomed to live with this uncertain feeling about God? If so, how could I possibly live without "fear for tomorrow" as I had lived in my past? My urgent need sent me asking, and each answer finally came to the truth, "I don't know but I believe."

I could understand the mother's grief and bewilderment who said, standing beside the casket of her child, "If I can believe this is the will of God, I can accept it"—only to have the pastor say, "But this isn't the will of God." How could he know that for sure when no minister I met could give me any such answer. Oh, sometimes I got such an answer, but when I pressed on for the source of his certainty, I finally came to hear his reason, "Because I believe. . . ." Every person was reduced in his careful reason to resting on what he believed about God and what he had experienced of God. Did I have this same right?

I can understand the effort of preachers to get away from this terrible God of wrath who stands by ready to strike at the least provocation. But in the effort to rid us of this concept of Him, have we discarded too much? As I talked with Christians, I found most of them had a smiling, loving, kind Heavenly Father who sent the sunshine and showers—One who showered blessings upon us and who showed Himself in the tender violets and singing birds. So, when life surrounds you with these, you may be thankful and rejoice.

"What about grief and heartbreak, disappointment and loss?" Well, that is just too bad. Then my Christian friends seemed to have a God who put a big hood over His head and waited until the storm was over. He'd peep out to be sure the damage was finished. Then, when all was clear, knowing the storm had passed, He'd bravely march out and see the mess it had left. He'd go to work. Never fear! No doubt! Out of the wreck He can bring good.

This kind of God wasn't big enough for me. I needed a God like the One St. Paul wrote about to the Philippian church, a God who is "... the master of everything that is." Feeling the greatness of such a God, Paul could write without self-pity, "They know that God has set me here in prison to defend our right to preach the gospel" (3:21; 1:16, Phillips).

"Oh no, Paul, don't say that! Surely you wouldn't infer that God had anything to do with your being in prison. Those wicked soldiers put you in prison. God just decided that since you were already there He'd make the best of it."

How I wished Paul could answer my question. Yet, as I reread his letter to the Philippians, I found there was some questioning, even then, about the kind of preaching being done. Paul discussed it for a while but didn't answer the question. Finally, he said, "But what does it matter? . . . It all accords with my own earnest wishes and hopes which are that. . . . I should honor Christ with the utmost boldness by the way I live, whether that means I am to face death or to go on living. For living to me means simply 'Christ,' and if I die I should merely gain more of him" (Phil. 1:18-21, Phillips). This is no idle statement from Paul. He knew death could be at any moment a reality. Yet he said something else that is rather shocking, "You are given, in this battle, the privilege not merely of believing in Christ but also of suffering for his sake" (Phil. 1:29, Phillips). Could the God who gives me the privilege of life with all its joys, be the same God who gives me life with all its sufferings?

I needed a faith in a God that not only held me while I was in the dark but gave me a light of hope for tomorrow. I needed, like Paul, to "leave the past behind and with hands outstretched to whatever lies ahead . . . go straight for the goal" (Phil. 3:13, Phillips) . But I could not find this faith as long as my God was simply cleaning up the past and not out there in the future. Would I ever find it as long as I tried to stretch my faith to cover everyone else's doubts?

Just as I had seen God guide and direct Burleigh, just as I had seen Burleigh hear and obey this direction, I could really believe that August 4th was no exception. I don't understand how, nor do I have to, but I can see the love of God surrounding Burleigh, screening all ill from him. Only when God in His wisdom parted the curtain did Burleigh land the plane.

How tragic it would have been had all the martyrs in Congo been black. What witness would the total church have if all the white martyrs had been Catholic? What political influence would have existed if no Americans were lost? What word for devotion would there have been if only Americans of small churches or independent boards had given their lives?

One by one these questions came to me. Then I saw my first pattern. Burleigh was the white, Protestant, American from a large church who joined the rank of Martyrs.

Not only that, he was the most widely known missionary, not only in Batetela Land, but among the Presbyterians and Southern Congo Missions as well. His service as mission pilot and his patient spirit had endeared him to those who knew him.

It might even distress some of my friends, but I could believe that God needed a witness and carefully chose one of the best He could find.

While listening one day to the tape recording of Burleigh's funeral I heard the Congolese pastor say, with tears in his voice, "God did not promise Uwandj Utshudia Koi that this would not happen to him when he said 'Go ye into all the world.' "

Suddenly it dawned upon me that I had felt He had. There had been too many times that, in the midst of chaos and uncertainty, I had quoted that verse with the promise "Lo, I am with you alway, even unto the end of the world." This promise had calmed my fears. Somehow I had felt safe. Harm could not reach me. Christ was there. Now I faced a reality—Burleigh had not been protected.

When Burleigh's testament had first come to me, I had glanced at it with its blood stains and then carefully put it away. But now, months later, I had an urge to get it out. As I thumbed slowly through the pages it fell open to the page of the great missionary commission. I read, "Now the eleven disciples went to Galilee, to the mountain to which Jesus had directed them. And when they saw him they worshiped him; but some doubted" (Matt. 28:16, 17, RSV).

They had fears too, I thought. I wondered if they were afraid of what might happen to them. If Jesus was leaving, who would rebuke the storms, cast out demons, be their voice of authority? Jesus must have sensed their fears and doubts, for He "came and said to them, 'All authority in heaven and on earth has been given to me. Go therefore and make disciples of all nations . . .'" (Matt. 28:18, 19, RSV).

How wonderful the disciples must have felt—how brave and strong when they heard that strong voice ringing out above their heads, "Lo I am with you always, to the close of the age."

Jesus had never deceived them. He always kept every promise—He would keep this one. They had no fear—they went with courage across their part of the known world and into distant lands. In my imagination I could see them going, turning the world upside down. But then what happened?

Tradition tells us that ten of those eleven disciples died martyrs—most of them on foreign soil. Pastor Luhaka was right. God did not promise Burleigh safety but He did promise never to leave him.

VI.

"PLANS OF WELFARE . . . NOT OF CALAMITY"

"GOD IS PREPARING YOU for that which He is preparing for you," I heard a friend say. I needed desperately to feel this had been true. As I looked back I could see God's hand moving. Now, with the loss of Burleigh, my pattern of life was so completely shattered that I needed to find something from my own past, apart from Burleigh, that was being woven into my present. My book, *Appointment Congo* became that linking thread.

"How soon after Burleigh's death did you begin your book?" I am often asked.

"Two years before his death," I answer. I usually receive a startled reaction. But it is true. I actually began writing the book in 1962. I had never dreamed of writing so I was not a frustrated author. I had written articles for the *African Christian Advocate* with the encouragment of Mrs. Esma Booth, my bishop's wife and a successful writer in her own right. Yet I actually felt afraid to put my thoughts down in such an evident way that others could see.

I had enjoyed writing letters and often found them quoted in articles or reports given by officials of the Methodist Board of Missions. But I felt no need to write for the world to read—I had nothing to say.

While on our second furlough, in 1961, friends began to urge me to write. As I sat visiting and sharing our experiences, friends again and again insisted, "Virginia, you must write these down. I'd just love a book of these experiences."

I gave it some thought, but never having written, I couldn't seem to get an inspiration collected so that I could take hold of it and begin work.

Then Burleigh returned with David and Paul to Congo leaving Margaret Ann and me in the States until it was declared "safe." We had no idea how long this would be. We were going to live with my parents and I would be speaking some, but even those engagements were limited because of my uncertain future.

The morning Burleigh kissed me goodbye at the furloughed missionary conference and left for Congo, I went back to my room with a most desolate feeling. It seemed my heart had gone to Congo and left my body behind. I had nothing to do to fill my lonely days.

As I prayed, my greatest concern was for courage to live through the next few days and weeks. I didn't want to be a "weeping widow," but I needed strength to accept what both Burleigh and I had felt was God's will for our lives. I for control more than anything else. My heart became quiet and I felt God had answered my prayer.

I went down to breakfast and, as I came down the stairs, I saw immediately a group of my Congo missionary friends. They began to ask, "What time did Burleigh leave?" I started to answer with great control and suddenly tears began to flow. As I wiped them away, I smiled and said, "Well, I prayed for God to dry my tears. I guess I'll just have to smile through them."

"Smiling Through Tears" flashed upon my mind. That would be my book! I would write the joys and heartbreaks of being a missionary. I suddenly wanted the world to know that being a missionary was not a sad, doleful, serious business, but that there were joys and excitement in it. But most of all there were even smiles in our tears. At last I had an inspiration that I could grasp.

My mother had saved more than 650 letters which I had written home during my ten years on the field. These I could use as reminders. Margaret Ann and I went with my parents to Pine Mountain, Georgia, for a two-week vacation. We rented a cottage at Roosevelt Inn where I could sit out on the stone terrace and look over the valley. I began by arranging the letters in chronological order and then I started reading them. As I read, I noted the experiences I felt were significant and listed them in a notebook. With my long list compiled, I rearranged my listings according to subjects and began writing.

Slowly, in longhand, I recounted these experiences, living again every detail. My heart was so much in Congo that I found that the smallest detail I could remember was like a nugget of joy discovered anew. The fact that Burleigh was once again seeing and living among many of these same scenes drew me to join him in my imagination, fired by memories.

As I wrote, my experiences were such a part of my life that I could not judge them. I could not realize their meaning to anyone else. But Mother and Dad were there for that purpose. From time to time one of them would walk out to see if I had finished another chapter. To my surprise I realized a subtle pressure. They were really eager to read the next chapter. "But they are my parents," I rationalized. "It is only natural that they would be interested."

With my manuscript finished, I returned to Tallahassee. But the story was still so personal I could not decide to attempt to publish it. Then a friend asked to read it. His position at Florida State University gave him many connections with qualified judges of the merits of my manuscript. It was only a few days until I had all the encouragement I needed—even the volunteering of a professional typist to do the finished manuscript. I decided to have three copies made —one for each of our children, should the book never be published.

Before the final typing was completed, I received my anticipated clearance to go to Congo. "Never mind," my interested friend said. "I'll see it through to the publisher."

He not only did this but his interest created an interest in his Sunday school class. They paid for all the typing.

In Congo, my life was so busy I almost forgot about the book. Then came a most interesting letter from the publisher saying they had seriously considered the manuscript but had decided it did not fit into their plans. They did, however, recommend that I send it to another publisher. Since I was in Congo they would be glad to forward it on for me if I would advise them to do so. I picked out another publisher at random and answered the letter.

Another wait—yet I felt no anxiety at all regarding the book. Then came a letter excusing the delay but again after much deliberation they had rejected the manuscript. They had returned it to my American address but closed by saying, "We trust that you will continue to seek a publisher."

With no experience, this encouragement was totally lost on me. I interpreted it as saying, "We don't want it but hope you can find someone desperate enough to take it." It had run its course so far as I was concerned. Yet I was amazed! I felt not one tinge of disappointment.

This news had arrived on Sunday morning with our weekly mail. As we were walking home from church, Burleigh asked if I was hiding a disappointment so I mentioned the rejection.

"You know, it's strange," I said, "but I have the deepest feeling that some day I'll write a book and all this will be in it. The time is just not right now."

In a teasing manner and yet to comfort me, Burleigh put his arm around my shoulder squeezing me against him and said, "Who knows? Some day I might even do something to be famous and you couldn't keep from telling about me." Little did he dream of how prophetic he was. It was only one year later that I had the compelling urge to tell the world Burleigh's story. This did not come immediately upon his death but several months later.

When I enrolled at Scarritt College in Nashville, I did not know what I wanted to study. To be honest I was at Scarritt because I had felt so definitely impressed that I should go there. Just why I should choose Scarritt or what I should prepare to do was not clear. I wanted to stay in some church-related vocation. Returning to Congo with my twelve-year-old, Margaret Ann, was out of the question. Sensing my indecision, my advisor suggested that I simply take subjects that interested me and not consider requirements or electives. I chose two that had this appeal. When I named those she said, "That's fine but both of these are among the most difficult we have. I'd suggest you select a little easier course for the third one."

I sat down to carefully examine the catalogue. It was hard to know what might be easier and anything I thought suited this requirement didn't appeal to me. Then I noticed "Writing for Religious Publications." That struck a note. No matter what the demands of such a course it wouldn't be memory work so I chose this subject.

In the presentation of the course, the instructor explained that, after a few weeks of assigned writings, each student would begin his own project of directed writing. He asked around the class what special interest each one had. I hadn't really given the project any serious thought, but as I listened to the various interests and writing experiences of my class-mates, I remembered my efforts in "Smiling Through Tears." The class knew of my recent loss so when my turn came I said, "I'd like to write Burleigh's story."

Maybe my own feeling of uncertainty interpreted the response of the class but I definitely did not feel any en-thusiasm in their response to this suggestion. Knowing I had such a limited experience in writing, they had reason to feel this was just another widow with emotions she needed to express. They were sympathetic if not enthusiastic. For lack of encouragement I dismissed the idea. I'd decide on something else later on.

As the weeks passed, I received baskets full of mail. Letters and cards came from all over the world. Many en-closed newspaper clippings telling of Burleigh's death. Again and again I read the word "Martyr." Headlines read, "Local Man Martyred" or "Missionary Martyred" or "Methodist Martyr" or "Blood of a Modern Martyr." The image of a martyr just didn't seem to fit Burleigh. It portrayed to me the picture of a poor, lonely man, deserted by friends, being led to his death.

I often recalled so vividly our days in the chaotic Congo after independence. To die a martyr seemed to me a rather glorious escape from all the tensions we had endured. I had remarked as much to Burleigh. Very seriously he had an-swered, "You cannot die a martyr for a cause you did not live for."

There began to grow in my heart a desire to tell the world that Burleigh had lived! It was the way he had lived that made him a martyr, not the fact that he was the victim of a murder. I wanted my children, especially the youngest, Margaret Ann, to have my memories of this wonderful life. And then there would someday be grandchildren who would never know Burleigh in life but must not be cheated of this part of their heritage.

But the inspiration did not yet take fire.

I wrote the assignments. My instructor's comments were gracious at times, severely critical at others. Then I did one in dialogue. We were to write a conversation, letting the characters describe a situation. I found my inspiration when Margaret Ann and I went to Morrison's Cafeteria for Sunday dinner. The waiting line reached outside into the unshaded parking lot. In front of us were a couple. He did not want to eat there. She did. Such a conversation we heard!

I wrote up the conversation for my class assignment and as a result my teacher suddenly became very interested in my writing. "You have a conversational style which is natural," he told me. When I bravely brought out "Smiling Through Tears" for him to read, he realized that I already had a good beginning. I took that manuscript and literally cut it up into anecdotes. I arranged these back into chronological order and began to fill in the story.

What a wealth of material there was in that manuscript! What a blessing it increasingly became to me. I could never have read the letters in 1964 as I had in 1962. Reading Burleigh's name over and over would have been too painful. Yet, I had already taken the real message from the letters. I had also taken many humorous incidents which I might have missed in the midst of grief.

Even with this good beginning, I still needed encouragement. At times it seemed presumptuous on my part to even imagine I could write a book. Here I found my teacher, Ben Logan, the instrument of God's providence. He would read and criticize. He seemed to sense just how much criticism I could take. Often he would approve a chapter, then later suggest I look at it again. I wrote and rewrote, lived again and again my life, pouring out my heart on paper. I realized just how blessed my life had been to have lived those twenty-two years with Burleigh. The writing was real therapy for me and I realized it was.

Writing the book was only part of the job. I had to find a publisher. With five chapters finished I sent those to a publisher with my projected outline for the rest. The editor responded most favorably requesting that I complete and resubmit the final manuscript. Experienced writers assured me that I had it made if I could maintain the same standard, so when it was completed, I mailed it with great expectations. No reply came. I endured painful weeks of waiting before I finally called, but I could get no decision. The publisher was not rejecting it, just holding it. Again Ben Logan became my advisor. He called to represent me and check on my interpretation of the decision. To his surprise, he found I was correct so he requested my manuscript be returned. It took a second urgent request before the manuscript was once again home.

So it went through three more publishers. Each time it was seriously considered. Each time encouraging phone calls and then finally a rejection notice. By the third ordeal I was beginning to feel the strain. The last one had been the most encouraging. The publisher was honestly interested but needed approval from the Methodist Board of Missions that it was a fair presentation from their standpoint. I had assurance that this would be given and it was—but too late to save the manuscript. Once again I had my manuscript home.

At that time I had more pressing matters to attend to, so I simply laid the manuscript aside until I felt more interest in it. Several days later during my early morning prayer time, I found the manuscript coming to my mind. As I talked with God about it, I could honestly say, "I did not write it for fame or fortune."

So far as I was concerned, my personal reasons for writing the story had been fulfilled. My children had it recorded. I had received my needed therapy. If the book had a ministry beyond us to others, then this was in God's providence. Every effort I had made had failed. I did not know what more I could do. I prayed for guidance but none came. I opened my desk drawer, reached over and took the manuscript and dropped it into the drawer, praying as I did, "Father, I release this into Your care and will. If you want it published, then You know how to bring this to pass. It is Yours."

A great peace flooded my heart. I was leaving my concern with the manuscript.

Only a few days later I was attending a tea at Scarritt College. Mrs. Leonard Wolcott, wife of the professor of missions and herself a gifted writer, came to me. "What has happened to your manuscript?" she asked.

I was tempted not to be really honest. It might seem foolish to expect anything to happen with a manuscript lying in a dresser drawer. Yet, I thought, "It doesn't take courage to witness to faith after everything has worked out. It is when the manuscript is still lying there that it takes courage to say, 'I'm trusting God.' "

Pulling together my courage, I told her just what had happened. Instead of looking shocked at such stupidity she said, "You know, I believe with you that it will be published."

Although she had not seen the manuscript she had heard from others who had read it that it did have value. Little did either of us realize how important our casual conversation was. The next morning Mrs. Wolcott went to Birmingham for a Christian education meeting. She was riding in a taxi with Dr. Mary Alice Jones and a gentleman whom she did not know who was discussing with Dr. Jones the publishing of some books by Rand McNally and Company.

Though Mrs. Wolcott knew Dr. Jones well, she did not realize that she was a consulting editor for Rand McNally. Overhearing their conversation Mrs. Wolcott asked the fatal question, "Have you considered publishing Virginia Law's book?"

Dr. Jones had met me, she knew the circumstances of my

life, so she was interested in what she heard about the book. That evening she wrote a note in longhand asking me if I would submit my manuscript for Rand McNally's consideration. When this note arrived, my heart leaped with amazement; hadn't God done exactly what I really had asked? I could never forget He had worked a miracle.

As we edited the final manuscript I came to know and appreciate Dr. Jones. She shared with me that one of her friends had asked, "How can two people so strong willed work so pleasantly on a manuscript?" This friend knew that authors and editors often have problems. She didn't realize that I really didn't feel any concern. I was trusting God to guide her as I felt He was guiding me. There was only one time I had felt uneasy about a change and later we reversed the decision without my having voiced my objection.

We saw amazing things as the book progressed. The greatest was in the delays which eventually pushed back publication date by three months. Even after I had read and approved the final galleys there were delays. Because of pressures to get copies out for special conferences, Rand McNally decided to run dummy copies with about ten pages of print and a few pictures; the rest would be blank pages to make the size. These were to be shown at conferences and orders taken for the completed book. I was away on a trip when a few dummies arrived. My son Paul looked at one and called me long distance. On the very first page he had found a terrible mistake. It read, "It was 1962, two years after Congo's Independence." The date should have been 1964. This really was a glaring error that I had missed.

When I called Dr. Jones, she was distressed because she was sure the book had already gone to press. She called Rand McNally and was referred from one desk to another as her call traced the route of the manuscript. Finally she reached the last desk. She explained her distress only to hear, "What?" A long pause, and then, "Can you believe it? A messenger is now standing at my desk, waiting for me to hand him the manuscript."

She made the correction and before they finished their conversation the corrected book began to roll on the press. *Appointment Congo* came off the press a beautiful printed and bound book, a real credit to Burleigh. But more than this, it was for me the real link between my present and my past. It became the thread moving on into my future. God had prepared me for what was to come in my life.

This thought could bring great comfort to me, yet I still needed a confidence that I could put my weight down upon. Viewing the past wasn't enough. I was still concerned about my future.

Reading a devotional book one morning I found a verse of Scripture quoted which I had never seen or heard before. It broke upon my mind like a bright light. Then it settled upon my heart as my very own promise from God. Every day since then I have found that the Holy Spirit affirms to me this special promise: "I know the plans which I am planning for you, plans of welfare and not of calamity, to give you a future and a hope" (Jer. 29:11, Rotherham).*

---

* Joseph B. Rotherham, *The Emphasized Bible* (Grand Rapids: Kregel Publications, 1959).

VII.

𝒮

NEW IDENTITY

IN THE MONTHS after Burleigh's death, I was finding my faith and trust being restored.

Then, as *Appointment Congo* began to develop, I could see that not only had God guided Burleigh but He was guiding me, too. He had actually been preparing me for that which He was preparing for me.

It was really shocking, at 42 years of age, to suddenly discover your unique gift from God. This is not to say that through the years I had suffered from an inferiority complex. I had always made the honor roll in school. I had thought this was my gift. After I married, I loved to cook and sew and do anything around my home. Then I thought that just being Burleigh's wife, the mother of three children, and being able to create a happy comfortable home was my gift. None of these was very impressive but this didn't bother me at all. I was happy and fulfilled and asked nothing more of life.

But now this wonderful husband was gone. I couldn't

be his wife. Two of my children were in college contemplating marriage. Only Margaret Ann was left. My role as mother was fast disappearing. I seemed to be losing, along with everything else, even that part of my personality that I felt was really me.

I could not really appreciate then what had happened to me. The person who ate and slept didn't seem real. The Virginia I knew seemed to have been destroyed. I only knew that I felt detached and at sea.

There was a strong temptation to turn and attach myself to those wonderful children, especially to my sons. Yet, I knew that either I would succeed and ruin their chances of finding their own life mates and happiness or that they would resist and I would be hurt.

Too many widows in their loss of identity as a wife have clung to their children destructively. I simply refused to create yet another problem for me and for my children. It was rather late in life, but I knew I needed some self-identity that didn't depend on anyone else.

In the midst of publishing my first book, I received a phone call asking if an anthropologist could see the notes from which my book was written.

"What notes?" I asked.

"The notes you took in Congo . . . maybe your diary," the caller said.

"I'm sorry but I don't have any notes or diary," I answered.

"No notes or diary? How in the world did you write such descriptive details without notes?" he asked.

"Out of my head," I had to reply. I went on and explained that I had referred to Mother's letters back in 1962 but only to make note of the incident. I had not even copied any of the details then for my initial writing. I had simply sat down at the typewriter, flipped an imaginary gear and out of my subconscious mind seemed to flow all the smallest details in perfect order. His utter amazement at my sense of observation made me stop and reflect.

As a child I had seen everything that went on around me. My parents and neighbors could not keep anything from my watchful eye. I remember my painful distress when, at an early age, I was told, "Aw, you didn't see that."

Is it possible for my mind to see so clearly something my eyes don't really see? I had wondered. Sometimes, it would later be revealed that I had actually seen it but no one ever seemed to remember to apologize for wrongly judging my observation.

As I grew into adolescence my ability to remember details presented another problem. Any detail the rest didn't remember was assumed to be added on for the benefit of the story. I was often made to think that what I recounted was not quite truthful since it contained more details than anyone else could remember.

By the time I had reached adulthood my sense of observation had sharpened so that I saw not only the big, obvious details but also the fleeting glance, the twitch of an eye, the gesture of a hand, the multitude of emotional reflex expressions. Now my observation was considered not only unbelievable and untruthful, but even worse, people thought me nosey. I just plain knew too much!

There must certainly be something wrong with me, I thought, to see so much, so clearly, and to remember it so well when no one else seemed to see anything.

As a child, in addition to observing everything about me, I further distressed my parents by telling what I had seen. I was an incessant chatterbox. I just loved words; not big words but simple little words. I loved the way words would fit together. I could take one sentence and play a game all alone seeing how many different ways I could use it. Naturally this would distress my parents. With six children there was a limit to how much repetition they could stand.

I would say something at the table, then pause only a moment and tell it again. In the midst of six noisy children I once announced, "Mary Sue has a beautiful new bike from her daddy for her birthday."

"She does," came the noncommittal reply. A few moments' pause and another try. "Mary Sue's daddy gave her a beautiful new bike for her birthday."

"Yeah." Yet another try—"Mary Sue's birthday present from her daddy is a beautiful new bike."

Now, really, that was enough, and the normal response came, "Yes, yes, we hear you. Three times now you've told us the same thing!"

"Not really," I said in utter sincerity. "I didn't say the same thing."

To my childish mind each sentence was a completely new creation. Is it any wonder, though, that I spent most of my childhood being told, "Please be quiet"?

Then I was into my teens, where talents are so important. My best friend could play the piano and organ beautifully. She was always invited to special banquets to play. Another friend sang and she went singing her way. Yet another friend studied "Expression" and could recite clever monologues. As for me, well, I could wait tables or work in the kitchen, so I was always invited for that.

Dating was so important! On one occasion when boys were choosing their partners for a youth picnic, a nice boy called out, "I'll take Virginia. She makes the best potato salad." Hardly a compliment in that context.

A handsome young fellow was at this time really the catch of the ball—all the girls had their eyes on him. One day my phone rang. He was calling to invite me up to his house to make candy that evening and listen to "Hit Parade." I didn't think I could go but he kept insisting so, that I was curious. "Why are you so insistent that I come?" I asked.

"Well, to be frank, Mother says we can't have it unless you come," he said.

Now my curiosity was high. "Why does she say that?"

"Because she knows you'll see that the kitchen is left clean," came the truth. Again, less than a compliment under the circumstances. Is it any wonder I grew up with the self-image of housekeeping being my unique talent?

When I got to Congo I thought perhaps I could develop some talent which the world judged of value. I had studied enough piano so that I could play hymns for my own needs. And in Congo the musical standards were not too high. At early prayers one morning, our regular pianist was absent. We sang the first song without the piano, but not very well, I thought. When the leader announced the second hymn, I decided to play it for them. By the time I was seated and ready, they had completed the first verse. With the second verse I joined them, playing quite well, I thought. At the end of the verse the leader motioned for a pause, then solemnly announced, "We'll now sing the third verse without the piano."

I knew then that even in Congo, piano playing was not my talent. Perhaps I had to know what I wasn't before I could know the real me.

But I had problems with the real me. I would be in a group of perhaps ten people, and we'd all be talking, saying approximately the same thing. Later, I'd hear someone say, "Virginia said . . ." and they would quote me perfectly. All ten people had been a part of the conversation? Then why single me out? At times I was afraid that I was the only person expressing myself—that I was being forward and pushy.

But it was this ability—this quality which has turned out to be the real me. When *Appointment Congo* was being published, an editor remarked to me, "You have the most unique way of expressing yourself." I couldn't see it and still don't, but I valued his judgment. Then the book was off the press, and everywhere I went people said, "I feel like I know you. Your book sounds just like you and no one else." Is it possible that all those reruns my poor family listened to are now paying off?

When people come to me and say, "I'll never forget what you said," and quote me exactly, I can see how God is using my ability to put my thoughts "in a nutshell." That was what I was doing before, but I couldn't realize it.

Forty-two years old and shaken to the foundations before I really discovered my own self-identity! And then I couldn't just stop with the discovery. The talents had to be developed. I had to learn not to tell everything I saw—even a gifted pianist has to learn *when* to play and when *not* to. I had to learn to be careful, not to say what I thought when being quoted might hurt someone else. Every art demands discipline.

But perhaps the most difficult part was learning to accept this Virginia who existed apart from Burleigh or any other person. Dr. E. Stanley Jones once said to a group of missionaries, "To love your neighbor you must first love yourself." This idea seemed strange to me, for I had always felt that loving my neighbor meant renouncing myself. Now I found that I was being driven to affirm myself. I did not plan to do this. I'm not sure I wanted it. But the thread that linked my past to my present was woven out of that which was uniquely Virginia.

No longer was I Burleigh Law's wife. I was Virginia Law, a separate person—alone. It was a terrifying identity.

I know of no words to describe that terrible, incomplete feeling that fills a person when he loses the companion who has come to be part of his very soul. I don't know the words but do I really need them? If you have experienced the feeling, you know the agony of it; if you haven't, then nothing I could write would make you feel it.

In my grief I did not fully realize what had happened

to me. When I saw how desperately some widows clung to their married name I wondered why. I found a widow one day near hysterics because someone had written her a letter addressed to Mrs. Mary instead of Mrs. John. "They are taking away the only thing I have left," she wailed.

I might have been tempted to say, "how stupid," since I knew she was better situated financially than most women; but I wasn't tempted. Uneasily I sensed that, although I hadn't gone into hysterics, I had resisted having to use my legal name, Virginia W. Law.

The circumstances of my life were such that I did not have to change many things since I was only beginning my life in the United States. Our bank account was listed as "Burleigh A. or Virginia W. Law." When I needed new checks I had no choice but to drop "Burleigh A." Living in Congo we had no charge accounts except at Rich's, in Atlanta, where we sent orders from time to time. Any new accounts I simply began in my own name. I was constantly making new friends who did not know Burleigh. Then *Appointment Congo* was published under my own name, and it was advantageous for any public appearance I made to be linked with my book. I had to use my own name.

Despite all of these pressures to use my own name, I discovered while shopping in Rich's, that my charge plate was still in Mrs. Burleigh Law's name. I did not have an item of identification, should the clerk ask for one. I later wrote back asking for a new plate.

I did not realize that I was still resisting so hard the loss of Burleigh's name. In fact, I did not even see my feeling as being one of resistance, and I'm not sure I would have accepted the fact had someone told me. True, this was something of Burleigh that I had, but I can now see that this name represented the "me" that I knew—my very self-image. The extension of this image that acted and interacted with other people was interwoven with this other person—Burleigh. When I felt that I was losing my very name—that which was me—I felt terribly threatened. I was being destroyed!

Nor did this revelation come in one great moment. I've never read anything in "advice to widows" that even speaks of this. Yet I have talked with hundreds of widows—some of whom have been widowed for years—who still defend viciously their use of their married name. Interestingly, I have observed that most often they are widows who were left financially independent and were not forced to get out and face a new, different world. But, again, I talk with widows who find themselves forced, as they accept new situations, to drop their married name. Again and again as they refer to their married name, I hear in one way or another the expression, "That is just me." In other words, "When I cease using my husband's name, I have ceased to exist."

It was only very slowly, as I found a new identity emerging, that I had the courage to let the old one go. I do not regret the keen sense of identity that I had with Burleigh. I'm sure that the joy and happiness that I had was possible because of my fulfillment in just being his wife and the mother of his children. I don't believe I would have added one moment of joy if along the way I had started to exert my ego and express this ego independently of him.

Even now I find it tragic to see the wreckage in homes and lives which wives have done expressing their egos. And I see quite a lot of it. I have yet to see a wife who radiates a deep sense of joy and fulfillment, with a sparkle in her eye when her husband comes near, who is crusading at the same time for her "ego-identity."

It is no accident that four times in the Bible we find "And the two shall become one flesh." There is a mysterious union between a truly loving husband and wife. How often through years together a man and wife will begin to look alike! How often she knows exactly what he thinks! They have even lost their individual physical identity to a certain degree, but they have found something more.

Yet discovering self-identity can be very frightening, especially when one has felt so very secure with another and then has lost the relationship. Just the thought of my being isolated in my own uniqueness—separated from any other person—created a disturbing sense of loneliness. Experienc-ing this without the physical presence of one with whom I had been so closely identified augmented my uneasiness. Yet, I doubt that it was unique. A sociologist once observed that he felt that the increasing pressure on teenagers to "go steady" was really a result of their basic need to belong or to identify with some other person. The herding instinct is assumed to be one of the basic drives of man, so any separa-tion from that with which I identified would be disturbing even though it was to find my real self. It just so happened that I did not have a choice in the matter. I had really lost my identity when I lost Burleigh.

In the year following Burleigh's death I was living through slow days, agonizing over and resisting change, cry-ing out in distress. Thus, I found Christ. I did not realize what was happening. The events simply came one day upon another. Yet I knew that He was there.

It was only when in my desperation I had really affirmed that I was not alone that I discovered what were my unique gifts apart from Burleigh. These gifts became the direction of my ministry, but my new sense of identity was not my security. This was based on my new relationship with Christ.

Looking back I don't really think I could have hastened realization. It was when the Holy Spirit took the words of a caller to trigger my mind, that I could reconstruct my past. Then I could see myself as I had never done. It was the Holy Spirit who affirmed the truth to my heart so I could accept it—"he will guide you into all truth" (John 16:13, KJV). This means even the truth about yourself and who you are.

Another factor in my discovering myself anew in Christ impressed me more and more. It was in giving myself away that I found myself.

I have said that at times it seemed presumptuous to think that I could write. This is really an understatement. Most of the time it seemed utterly stupid not only because of my lack of experience; who could possibly care about whether my children ate white ants or not? There was hardly a page I wrote that did not cause me to question the relevancy of the material. Again and again my friend Ben Logan would give the manuscript back to me saying "details." It was his painful prodding that made me open up and tell what I had really seen and experienced. I felt then that he was God's providence for my book, and even more that it was his prodding that made me open my heart so that the real Virginia could come forth.

Someone has said, "Only that which we give away truly becomes ours." If I had not attempted to give the world a book from behind the closed doors of my life, I would never so soon have found the new life.

"He that loseth his life . . . shall find it" (Matt. 10:39, KJV). This raises for me a serious question, "Does anyone ever find his true ego-self when he is seeking for it and exerting every effort for it?" Do you ever answer the question, "Who am I?" when you are running about asking it? I believe not. Self-discovery seems to me to be the serendipity of self-surrender or giving. Certainly it was in my case.

I discovered another amazing fact about finding myself in the midst of grief. My first glimpse of direction came when I turned to help another find her way.

A professor at Scarritt College for Christian Workers asked me one day, "Virginia, do you really realize what you have lost?"

I wasn't sure I understood his question. As I pondered, he began to elaborate. "You not only lost Burleigh, but you lost your home [he knew that the rebels had looted my Congo home], your friends are scattered, and your profession is gone. You are no longer a missionary."

I realized that all of that was gone but that was not my greatest loss. More than any of those, I had lost my place of service. For fourteen years, I had known the thrill of being involved in service to others. Many things I had been forced to do on the mission field seemed mundane and trivial at the time. Yet my overall life had been full of service.

In my distress one morning I cried out, "Lord Jesus, as if it isn't enough to have lost Burleigh, my home, my friends, my profession, to have lost my place to serve is even worse."

Then, in the midst of the agony that enveloped me, a strange quietness filled my heart. I had come to recognize this as His voice. Into my mind came the face of a girl I sat near in class. She was not a very pleasant person, and I had avoided her when possible, as I knew others did. Now I saw her real need for a friend.

"Oh no," I cried, "not her."

Yet her face would not leave me. I arose the next morning to go offer her sincere friendship. I discovered that what she really needed was a mother substitute. Her relationship with her mother had been tragic from her birth. Circumstances which she could not control or change had caused her to be rejected. Really all she needed was a "mother" to sit and talk to—and I had had good experience at that.

The girl often expressed her appreciation to me, but I had reason to thank her: it was in giving her a little time that I was finding a meaning for my life—a meaning which I had lost.

VIII.

VULNERABILITY

EVEN MORE FRIGHTENING than the loss of identity was the terrible feeling of vulnerability I had. After all these years of being cared for, I now faced the dark cold world alone. If my car needed repairs, I was the person who had to drive down to that dirty old greasy garage in a part of town I would never have visited alone. Not knowing one thing about cars only compounded my uneasiness which mounted into a fear that I might not get what I paid for in the deal. The kind council of friends to "watch out you don't get cheated" only confirmed my fears. Fortunately I was often able to see that my fears were usually ungrounded.

Yet I have discovered many widows who expend their total energies "protecting their interest." One widow I know has received and paid her gas bill for years in the ordinary way. Even when her husband lived she handled the household bills; he never bothered himself with such a care. But after he died she suddenly became suspicious that her meter isn't being read correctly. Although her husband had paid absolutely no attention to the reading, now that he is gone, she begins to feel vulnerable and to become suspicious.

One woman had had the same laundry man for twenty years. Twice a week he had stopped and often chatted both with her and her husband who was retired and, due to failing health, sat on the side porch near the kitchen. Both men were interested in hunting, and they would discuss where the doves were, the makes of guns, how hunting was that season.

Then the husband died. Only a few weeks later the laundry man made one of his regular calls at the widow's house and went on. He was busy with his route when his laundry received a distressing call—"My laundry man stole my husband's gun!"

The laundry owner could hardly believe this. A few minutes later a lawyer called to advise them that his client had reported a gun stolen by one of their delivery men. When the delivery man finally reached the laundry he was shocked. At first, he couldn't believe that such a report had come in. Then he recalled, "Why that gun was hanging this morning on the same rack it has been for years." Sure enough—when the manager went around he saw it as he knocked at the kitchen door.

There are many explanations but no real excuse for such a mistake. A widow, feeling vulnerable, was suspicious. Her suspicions had created her own basis for the accusation.

This feeling of vulnerability seemed always keen when I began to face myself in relation to others. This was especially a cause for uneasiness where men were concerned. Not only had I lost my sense of identity, but I had lost my sense of protection. Before, when I traveled, I had had Burleigh right there. Even if I went alone he usually saw me off and welcomed me home. No matter how separated we might be, or for how long, just the knowledge of his being in my life gave me a sense of security and protection. Now I did not have this! I felt terribly vulnerable! I found myself saying the Mrs. to my name louder than necessary. I seemed compelled to let the world know that I was married. Yet this was foreign to my usual way of acting.

Then I found people referring to me, even in my presence, as "that attractive, young widow." Now I knew I wasn't that pretty. I also knew people had not called me "that attractive Mrs. Law." And there was always the subtle reference to the "widow's problem," inferring that a poor widow is sure prey for any wolf that may be on the prowl.

At first I simply claimed the presence of Jesus if I felt any sense of uneasiness. When I could realize He was there I was once more comfortable. As time passed these prayers came further and further apart. My times of uneasiness were fewer until I rarely needed this prayer.

I had just begun to overcome my sense of uneasiness when I attended a banquet one evening and was seated by a very nice-looking minister about my age. I did not know anything about him except his name and church. We began to talk. He had gone through some very difficult experiences which he shared with me.

At every break in the banquet program he returned to our subject and picked up where he had stopped. In the course of many trials, his wife had discovered she had cancer. He commented, "I never really faced surrendering my wife to God until that night. I thought I had. But it wasn't until after hours of praying that I knew finally I had."

He moved on to another surrender he had made which was the point of his sharing. Hours later, after I had traveled miles to my next engagement, I crawled in bed. Remembering our conversation the thought suddenly struck, "I wonder if she died."

It had never once entered my mind at the time. I had enjoyed so much the depth of personal sharing and witness that I had lost any sense of his sex identity. I knew then that

God had heard my prayer. He had freed me from my haunting sense of being vulnerable and had given me his presence and security.

From this new feeling of security I could look honestly at my situation. I discovered that I wasn't in nearly as much danger as I had thought. While traveling, I met some of the nicest gentlemen I could ever meet. I almost hated to admit that I had not met anyone who hadn't been a gentleman. I came to realize that you are expected to have trouble if you are a widow.

Shocking, isn't it? But oh the accounts I've heard! That is, until I have indicated that I was really quite safe. Too many times to be mere chance my informant will look at me rather surprised and say, "You mean men don't make passes at you?"

"No, I'm afraid they don't."

"Maybe you just don't see them."

"Well, that could be. But I don't see them, and I'm just as safe as if they hadn't wasted their effort."

Now, I have to admit that there may be the office wolf wandering around, or the occasional man on the prowl, but on the whole, I have the feeling that Christian widows are being sold a bill of goods. We have let Hollywood create an image for us; we are fooled into thinking that if we have any femininity, any sex appeal, then we have to make every man we meet paw the ground. This very sense of expecting a pass creates an atmosphere to help produce one. Every such experience only makes preparation for the next one. Somewhere the vicious cycle must be broken. Either the widow comes to enjoy a potentially dangerous game or she withdraws in fear.

If you are one of those withdrawing in fear, I highly recommend that you claim the presence of Jesus around yourself and around the person who disturbs you. Then ask Jesus to give you a new image of yourself as an attractive and lovable person who is admired by men as you really wish to be in Christ.

I'm often asked by envious widows, "How do you travel with those men in the lay witness movement?" And I must explain that I do have some of the most wonderful friends among men that any widow could ever want, and lots of them too. Now, I've shared my secret but I also have proof that it works.

I do not wish to imply that what I have said makes you some piece of dead wood with never any sexual response—far from it. But it frees you from a fear that makes such responses seem both dangerous and threatening. When I am aware of any such response, I simply look up with my heart and say, "Thank you, Father, I'm still alive." This recognition of the emotion lifts it up where God's love can take it and change it into sparkle and personality instead of guilt.

I don't deliberately expose myself to movies or stories that are sexually provocative, yet I don't condemn or deny what are normal human emotions. I have also found that my deep need to love and be loved can find a real release in expressing my love for Jesus. Lying in bed alone I just tell Him how much I do love Him, how wonderful He has been to me, and I find that His love embraces me and I feel loved. It is really, after all, this deep feeling of being loved which brings release from frustration, not just the physical expression of love.

Being able to lift these emotions to Jesus frees me to be with and enjoy men as I did when I had Burleigh. The same rules of discreet conduct still hold as they did then, not because I'm a widow, but because I'm a Christian. I have a perfect freedom to go anywhere a married lady goes. The more I travel, the more I am convinced that only when His Spirit makes you free are you really free.

Not only are you free to live around men but you are

free to live away from them, too. When I was first alone,
friends would comment, "Oh, you'll marry again." I never
said I wouldn't but I resented their dismissal of my problems
with such an easy answer. Then I found that, even to me,
this seemed my only hope of ever finding a happy, fulfilled life.

There must be a general feeling that this is true, hence,
the nomenclature "desperate widow." I have often laughed
at a friend of mine who had been widowed for many years.
"Have you ever considered remarrying?" I asked her.

"Oh, yes," she said, "at first I would have married if I
could have found someone to measure up. I guess my yard-
stick was too long." She paused a moment and said, "And
now, well if he could just rock his own chair."

I was determined that a marriage would not be an attempted escape from grief. I would work through my grief
and then see what life offered.

Yet I saw in myself what I saw in many widows and what
one expressed to me. "You'll never live again, Virginia, you'll
only exist."

All my adult life had been lived married to Burleigh. I
had no experience in happiness outside of marriage. I could
not conceive of any real happiness existing apart from someone to share life with intimately as only a husband and wife
can. I rather accepted my doom as a poor, pitiful soul who
would go through life from forty-one until (if I was lucky)
sixty-five, just eating hay. So many widows I met only added
to this conviction. I must admit that one at a time widows
aren't too bad, perhaps even delightful, but much too often
two or more widows just add misery to misery.

I'm not sure just what started me to trying to find some
other answer. Even though I was complimented when asked,
"How do you stay single?" I had to admit, "I'm not having a
bit of trouble staying this way."

Maybe it was the statement I read which advised me there

were nine million widows in America. No matter how high my friends might rate me, I knew I wasn't a prize peach in such a glutted market.

I had always felt a certain sense of pity for any unmarried person. Because I knew such happiness and fulfillment in my own marriage, I couldn't imagine that one could find it outside of marriage. Again I had the attitude "What don't I know?"—"What don't I know about happiness?" Somewhere, however, it dawned upon me that this attitude is nonsense. Christ came that I might have abundant life and He didn't add the condition, "If you have a husband."

I was fortunate that I had come to know well a very lovely single lady in Congo. Burleigh was often a meal guest in our single friend's home when he flew to her station. He always enjoyed it. She had delightfully humorous stories of the early days of our mission. Often Burleigh would comment, "You know, I never stop there that I don't feel like I'm in a family."

What Burleigh really saw was her expression of completeness. This showed in the way her table was set . . . in the flowers always on the table . . . in the way she always dressed with some touch of femininity. Everything about her said, "I'm a woman." She had acquired no masculine traits. She made her contribution but she never competed with the men.

I asked her one day why she had never married. Without a trace of self-pity or sacrifice she answered, "Because I decided to be a missionary." She had no long story of disappointed lovers left weeping on America's shores as she set sail. She had simply made her decision to serve in Congo and that had been the price she had paid.

I knew that she had found real fulfillment in life and, if she could, I could, too. This was not shutting the door to any possibility of marriage. I would still pray that God would send into my life those people that I needed and those who needed me. If one of those should be a man who could love me and one I could love, so much the better. But I was not sitting, holding my breath until he came. I would try to find all the abundant life that Christ offered me.

IX.

DRAWING ON RESOURCES

"RESOURCES FOR LIVING THROUGH TRAGEDY" was the title assigned my discussion group at a Key Layman's Conference
sponsored by Emory University. Early one morning as I meditated about this session it suddenly occured to me to ask
myself, "If you have the resources, do you have real tragedy?"

I think not. Tragedy occurs when there are no resources.
That is not to say, however, that having resources eliminates
the hard and rough places of life. These resources are not
hastily gathered. They are all the painful steps in spiritual
growth and understanding gained through the years. They
are also the abundance of enlightment waiting in the Bible
for one to discover.

In the 14th chapter of St. John, Jesus is talking to the
disciples about going away. For about three years they had
followed Him. They even talked like Him. The group
around the fire at Caiaphas' house accused Peter, "Certainly
you are also one . . . your accent betrays you" (Matt. 26:73,
RSV) . They were His disciples. Their identity was based on

this relationship. But now He was talking about leaving.

To their troubled hearts Jesus says, "You must not let yourselves be distressed" (John 14:1, Phillips). Then, to further reassure them, He speaks of the place He will prepare for them. They know Jesus. They trust Him. Now they may be confident for He is the very Way to this place—the Father's house.

Yet this is another new, strange situation—this Father's House. Nothing is there to which those uneasy disciples can relate! But, one more step, and Christ reveals that His own identity is related to another. " . . . I am in the Father, and the Father in me" (John 14:11, KJV). Even Christ is living His life in relationship to someone else. In His prayer for these disciples He forever breaks the loneliness of self-identity. "Just as you, Father, live in me and I live in you, I am asking that they may live in us . . . I in them and you in me, that they may grow complete into one" (John 17:21, 23 Phillips).

He patiently told His disciples of the coming of the Holy Spirit. He was really saying to them, "I am not going to leave you alone in the world," (John 14:18, Phillips), even though He was removing Himself from their visual presence. Each of them would be forced to find his own unique selfhood but they need never fear for they would never really work alone.

Even in the isolation of discovering their self-identity they would realize that "I am in my Father, that you are in me, and I am in you" (John 14:20, Phillips). What a thought to drive away the haunting fear of having to isolate myself from all earthly attachments to truly find myself!

Could I really find what those disciples found? Luke tells us that after their Master was taken away, ". . . they worshipped Him, and returned to Jerusalem with great joy" (Luke 24:52, KJV). This joy was not attained at the end of their Christian life but was there from the beginning.

Christ in me became the recognized basis of my new security. It was not that I had not known Him for years. It was not that He had not been very present in my life. I guess it was simply that I had never come to a point of desperation at which I realized He really was all that I had. It is often just such a sense of desperation that brings a person to Christ in an initial encounter. This was not true for me. Someone has said, "God cannot do for you what you do not feel you need." Perhaps more accurately in my case, I could not fully appreciate what Christ was doing in and through me until I felt a desperate need. At that point, I realized that I not only had peace but what was more wonderful, I had the "Giver of Peace" Himself.

It was as if I had known for years that I had owned stock in some company but I wasn't concerned about the details. I knew where they were safely kept. I had gone about my business with confidence and made decisions courageously for I knew I had these. Then came the day when I lost everything else I owned. I went to the bank, opened the vault, lifted out the certificates—and only then discovered the great value of these stocks.

There is always a temptation to feel that if we know something or someone, we know all there is to know. I'm often reminded of an incident that happened when our son Paul was about five years old.

A missionary family with an eight-year-old daughter was returning to our Congo work from a year of French study. Traveling to their assignment, they stopped to lunch with us. At the table, we began to discuss the girl's experience in learning French. As is always true of children and languages, she had done better than her parents.

Turning to her, Paul asked, "Do you know *all* the French?"

Puzzled by his question, she looked at her mother who began to explain, "She knows all the French she needs, but not all the French there is. Just like you don't know all the English there is."

Rather shocked at such a comment, Paul turned and asked us, "What don't I know?"

Amusing, yet there was no way we could really tell him what he didn't know. He would later realize this for himself.

There had come a time in my life, while I was a missionary in Congo—certain that Jesus was the Lord of my life and knowing that I was giving my life in service to others—when I was forced to ask myself, "What don't I still know about Him?" The difference between Paul and me was that I realized there was yet a deeper, surer knowledge that I had not found.

Strange that it was an uneducated African woman who showed me my ignorance. Some years before Burleigh and I had moved to Lomela, Mama Dundja had walked from Lomela to Wembo Nyama—a 300-mile trip over winding forest paths strewn with roots and stubble. She had to wait for surgery and after the operation waited to recuperate before her walk home. For the nine months she stayed at the hospital, she attended the early morning worship service each day. During this time, she heard the story of Jesus and accepted Him as her Lord.

She returned home with a new Bible and a hymn book. She couldn't read or write but she could stop other people who could. From just listening, she memorized great portions of Scripture. She often had different sections mixed up, but somehow even that seemed all right.

Taking her little "Ekuli" drum, Mama Dundja would call the people together. Then unwrapping her precious Bible she would preach—without reading a word. The witness of this simple woman left no room for doubt about her life. In a culture where women have no real status, she was asked to witness the exchange of dowry more than any man. People said, "She won't lie."

I knew this and could not help but admire her. Every time we stopped at her village she would come rushing out, clapping her work-scarred hands, beaming with a radiant snaggled-toothed smile, and greet me, "Mama Uya Koi, do you love Jesus?"

"Why that greeting?" I wondered uneasily. Why doesn't she ask me how many pencils I gave the students, how much drugs I left at the dispensary, or even how many Bibles I sold on the way? There were so many questions she could have asked about what I was doing. And, after all, wasn't all this really done for Jesus? But she didn't seem to care what I had done. She wanted sincerely to hear my answer to the question, "Do you love Jesus?" This bothered me but I wasn't sure why nor concerned enough to seek the answer.

But there were other reasons for my uneasiness. There were just too many times that we were rushing on our way feeling too pressed for time to stop in her village which was located in a deep curve in the road; people approaching from any direction could not be seen until they had rounded the curve. We would come rushing around the curve carefully following the two-track road—yet there she would be—standing in one of the tracks! Of course, we would stop. We were never in such a hurry that we would run over her. Up to our car she would come, clapping, beaming and asking her question, "Mama Uya Koi, do you love Jesus?"

Then she would say, "I was down in my garden hoeing my corn and Uwandji Jesus told me, 'You better hurry, Mama Uya Koi is coming.' "

Catching a quick breath, she'd rush on, "I just laid down my hoe and ran all the way."

Then, smiling more broadly than ever, and looking toward the heavens, she would lift both of her hands up even with her radiant face and say, "Isn't Jesus wonderful?"

I'd smile with her—but not really. Deep within I felt a tinge of pity for her. Such a simple, uneducated woman. I knew better than this. *Jesus didn't tell her I was coming. He doesn't talk to people like that today. I'm sure there is some logical explanation for her knowing this.* Then I would set about to find what it could be.

In such a search, I was really handicapped. She didn't have a television or radio, telephone or telegraph, and not even drum messages can be sent in the heat of the day. As if those weren't enough obstacles, many times we had only decided an hour before to come her road. Certainly no one could have outrun us to bring her word! Still I would not be convinced.

Did I believe in Jesus? Certainly I did. My entire background had been very orthodox. Why I even believed in the Virgin Birth, and that was supposed to be the sure hallmark of people who believed in Jesus. I prayed, really prayed, and there was no doubt to me that my prayers were answered. By every test I knew Jesus was really the Lord of my life. Yet, here was a dimension of relationship with Him that made me uneasy. "It's just so naïve," I said. "With my education I've grown above that."

Months passed, however, with one experience reinforcing another; Mama Dundja had too good a batting average for it to be mere chance. Yet, when forced to face it, I would smile and thereby hope to hide my uneasiness.

Things finally reached a climax while we were meeting with the district pastors. There was a very serious problem in one of our multi-tribal congregations. For hours we discussed the situation until it became rather evident that we had exhausted our supply of "bright" solutions.

One of the pastors spoke up, "Why don't we just wait on this until tomorrow when Mama Dundja comes?"

I turned to him with a rather sickly smile to hide my real feelings and said, "Why? Do you think she will know the answer?"

Obviously not really sensing my question he answered

with sure confidence, *"Mete,* truly I know she will, for she talks with Uwandji Jesus."

With force his answer hit me! *Why does he expect her to know when I don't? Why, I'm 7,000 miles from home peddling answers! How impossible that Congolese who can't read or write would know more than I, an educated missionary!*

I must confess for honesty's sake that I went to bed that evening thinking, *I hope she doesn't know. He'll find out that Mama Dundja isn't so special, after all.*

The next morning she arrived. Again we gathered in a small stick and mud church. The head pastor turned to Mama Dundja and began to explain our problem. After only a few words she interrupted, "I know." Then, in the most unassuming way and yet with a voice of authority, she added, "Yesterday I was talking with Jesus and He told me . . . ."

There was the perfect answer! So simple, yet utterly inspired—and I knew it. No sneer, no tingle of pity, no haughty attitude was in my heart. I knew as deep a spiritual hunger as I will ever know. Deep in my soul I cried "Do you have to be uneducated? Do you have to be unable to read or write to know that kind of relationship? Can't someone who thinks and reasons—someone with a tendency to always be logical— know Jesus like that?"

At that moment I would have gladly exchanged all my culture and educational training for Mama Dundja's sense of personal identity with Christ. But I knew this was not the solution. The Apostle Paul, with more of both of these than I ever would have, had written "For to me to live is Christ . . . ." (Phil. 1:21, KJV).

From that day, I began to learn from this simple village woman. I asked her question after question and tried to hear what she said.

Strange as it may seem, I found that I was very comfortable with the whole concept of God as Father. He was so high and lifted up that I knew I would never reach His standard. I would relax visualizing Him looking down on my frailties and weaknesses.

But Jesus was another question. There was something about Him that held a measuring rod against me. He revealed my highest potential and where I failed to measure up. Mama Dundja's question, "Do you love Jesus?" made me uncomfortable, for just hearing it raised other questions. "If ye love me," Jesus had said, "Keep my commandments" (John 14:15, KJV). Then again, "This is my commandment, That ye love one another, as I have loved you" (John 15:12, KJV). His standard of love reveals my shame and insincerity.

Yet, even in the face of this painful revelation, I could not say, "This is impossible," for there was Mama Dundja. With all her human imperfections she had divine communion. I had looked upon her as one of those other sheep of whom Christ spoke in John 10:16. And truly she was, for she had heard His voice. That really seemed to be the secret of knowing Jesus. I would have to learn to recognize His voice.

There began a sincere search for a real communion with this Jesus Mama Dundja knew so intimately. How eternally grateful I have been that I did search, for after Burleigh's death, I don't believe I could have ever found my way through such a shattering of my physical environment if I could not have somehow heard Jesus speak. Left with this very real loss of that which I claimed as me, and forced to find myself in isolation, it was only natural that my seeking would turn to Jesus.

There was simply no word in my entire vocabulary that gave me the sense of a Presence like "Lord Jesus." I felt that He understood my distress. I did not feel alone for I was not alone.

I had now come to the place in my life where talking with Jesus no longer seemed a luxury. Before this I had prayed, but whether or not I would have admitted it, if I didn't pray it really wasn't too important. Now I had to know He was there. I had to have His courage to lift the shade to see if the sun would shine. I had to know that the decisions were not entirely mine. He would be there! I did not decide alone!

So, desperately at first, I did cling to Him. And in the midst of this I found a new sense of strength and peace welling up from deep within me.

As I began to heal emotionally I found myself full of fear—fear that I might discover my own identity apart from Jesus. I prayed a prayer that I still pray—"Lord Jesus, don't let me ever go back to the place where I think I can live without You." Jesus was my greatest resource—I could draw on Him.

X.

DEEP HEALING

LEARNING TO DRAW ON MY RESOURCES did not come in one week, nor even in one year. It progressed slowly over about three years.

In those years I was amazed at God's grace and guidance. I was amazed at myself and how brave I had been at times. Yet I was aware of striving to be brave.

There were just too many times when I had felt the weight of the load and had had to cry for God's reinforcement for my bridge. There were too many memories that brought tears to my eyes and a lump in my throat—tears that I did not shed and a lump I had to swallow. I was aware of this, but I thought a broken heart was the eternal burden of a widow. I decided I would just trust God for sufficient grace and try to suffer in silence.

But about two and one-half years after Burleigh's death, I had a very wonderful experience. A friend gave me a series of recorded tapes she had gotten from Agnes Sanford, an Episcopalian lady who speaks a great deal on spiritual healing. Quite by accident, I chose her talk on the "Healing of the Memories" to hear first.

After supper, I took a hot bath and, all relaxed, lay down to listen. Her message challenged me. I did not take notes but I remember how impressed I was as she spoke of how God's love could go back even in our subconscious mind and heal our wounds, how the child who was rejected but has forgotten this rejection can be healed in the heart, how guilt can be healed so that we don't remember it any more. What a message! And with every word I heard, my heart affirmed it as true!

I finished the tape and lay thinking. "If God can heal all those damaged emotions, why can't He heal heartbreak? Why can't He take away the pain of hurt? Why can't He control the tears before they rise? If He can reinforce me when I need it, I believe He can work before I need it."

The more I lay thinking, the deeper became my conviction that I was on the right track.

Then I began to face some probing questions. "Do you really want to be healed?" I knew that this is one of the first conditions to spiritual healing.

"Are you willing to really give up self-pity?" What a hard question! I thought I had done that, but painfully the Holy Spirit revealed to me the multitude of evidences that there was still more to be done.

"Are you willing totally to accept your loss and your widowhood?" Just a question and, yet, on careful scrutiny, I began to see many ways that I still resisted the loss of my identity with Burleigh and the acceptance of my new self.

As strange as it may seem, and it seemed strange to me then, I realized that my wedding band was definitely a resistance to this acceptance. I had immediately pulled off my band when I heard that Burleigh had been killed—I had never had it off since my wedding day. I didn't want the band to be a fetish. But I put it back on later and I kept wearing it—I heard such comments as, "When a widow takes off her wedding band, she's hunting a husband." I'd seen too many wearing their band and hunting just the same to think that comment was completely true. Every time I accepted a dinner date, I took the ring off in courtesy to the gentleman, but then back on it went—my status symbol.

I realized, however, that it was also definitely hindering my emotional healing. Each time I looked at it, I was reminded of an identity I had lost. My diamond was different —it reminded me of the love which I still had.

I could not come to any decision that night about my ring but I did feel that I must.

I knelt beside my bed and prayed. I believed that God could heal even heartbreak. I was willing to give up any self-pity if He would reveal it to me. I would do everything I could to accept myself as a widow. Then I simply prayed, "Lord Jesus, come and heal me." It was not a complicated prayer but it was completely honest and sincere. I did not feel any different. Yet, I felt confident that God would answer and I thanked Him.

Weeks passed and I had almost forgotten it when I was sitting in a big hotel lobby waiting for a ride. There is no place more lonely when you see that everyone else is with someone. Suddenly I felt exhilarated—just as if something wonderful was going to happen. My heart was lifted with joyful anticipation. Then I heard with my conscious ear what my subconscious mind had already registered. Through the doors of the lounge came a beautiful baritone voice singing "Because"—one of my wedding songs.

Once more in my memory I was standing waiting for the signal to march down the aisle to become Burleigh Law's bride. All the joy and love of that wonderful moment multiplied through the years flooded my heart. I had been healed! I had experienced the grace of God taking my deepest grief and creating my highest joy.

There were a multitude of evidences that this was true. Yet I still wore my wedding band. And I was more and more aware of it. I would try taking it off, but that finger seemed too painfully bare. I'd put it back on. This went on for several months—taking it off and putting it on. I could feel it blocking my total release to accept my healing. Finally one day, I got a lovely pearl and diamond ring. Immediately I had my engagement diamond sized for my right hand and placed my wedding band in my dresser drawer. I felt then that I had fully accepted my healing and my widowhood.

I am not crusading against widows wearing their wedding bands. Yours may be no hindrance to your deep emotional healing, but mine was. And I wanted badly enough to be healed to give up anything to have it.

What a difference this experience made in all of my life! The heartbreak was gone. I could enjoy memories and share experiences freely. If tears did come they didn't hurt anyone. *Why didn't I find this sooner?* I wondered. I really felt kind of peeved at God that He hadn't sent me that tape months or even at least a year sooner.

Perhaps to keep me from rushing out to witness to every widow I see, God revealed to me that my experience was like a deep hip wound I once had in Congo. I had developed a deep abscess in my hip after a pentamidine shot for sleeping sickness. Our doctors had lanced it but had had to cut very deep. I was in bed for several days before I was able to be up and about. After I got up, my nurse went away for a few days. When she returned she asked me, "Did Doctor Bob take the drain out?" I didn't know, but she decided he must have.

My hip healed and I went home. Months later I had another abscess. Dr. Bob had not taken the drain out. It had slipped down deep into the wound. My hip had healed on the surface where the painful nerves were, but not down deep.

This parable showed me that I had needed all that time to achieve deep emotional healing. There was much that I had to face— much I had to learn. Every experience, every insight, every ray of understanding had been absolutely necessary for me to heal at those deep, deep levels. When I was ready, my surface wound, where most of my pain was felt, was healed. Only when I was ready could this happen.

I'm sure God did not want me giving witness to people in grief who were not ready, without telling them of the whole painful process. Only to a few people have I shared this and then only when I had time to give it in detail.

Now I have really, for the first time, felt that I should relate my experience, but you can see all that went before my healing. I do not offer any quick, easy way out of grief and heartbreak, but I do offer hope.

I remember too well the widow who said to me, "I hate to tell you, Virginia, but it gets worse as time goes on." "It can't get any worse," I cried out to God. "I can't take it." Then quietly I remembered "underneath are the everlasting arms."

The psalmist's words bring hope to the hopeless: "I waited patiently for the Lord; and he inclined unto me, and heard my cry. He brought me up also out of an horrible pit, out of the miry clay, and set my feet upon a rock, and established my goings. And he hath put a new song in my mouth, even praise unto our God. . . ." (Ps. 40:1-3, KJV) .

Only through God's deep-healing process could I rise above the hurt. Only through His grace could the real Virginia Law stand.

XI.

NO BITTERNESS

"How have you overcome bitterness?" asked a radio interviewer who had met me only minutes before.

His question stumped me for a moment. I had never really felt any bitterness. Strange, I couldn't actually remember having had to pray for forgiveness. As I tried to surrender myself to Christ, to find His will and purpose in my grief and in my own life, forgiveness just seemed to come.

There had been a brief moment, perhaps, of bitterness. The first letter we received which gave details of Burleigh's death told how he had said, "Don't blame him [meaning the rebel], he didn't understand me." My immediate reaction was, "Why did Burleigh say that? You must blame him. That soldier was not shooting an automatic. He had to load his gun before every shot. He intended to kill Burleigh."

Fortunately, I did not say anything. I handed the letter to David who read it, then looked up at me in amazement, "Gee, Dad forgave him! If Dad can, I sure can."

David had expressed the attitude of all three of my

children. As a family, we learned that forgiveness was not
something we worked to produce, but it seemed to be a
natural fruit of the Spirit of Christ which we were seeking
as we tried to find God's will.

"How did you know I wasn't bitter?" I asked my interviewer later. I was suddenly impressed that he had said,
"You have overcome bitterness," not "Have you overcome?"

"Oh," he said, "I interview too many bitter people. I
could tell by the light in your eyes."

Pondering over his reply I realized that I had seen the
same thing. So many times I had looked at a person and
seen, etched in his face, lines of bitterness.

For us to find forgiveness in our hearts has been wonderful, but for Burleigh to find it was a miracle. I still marvel
that, lying by his plane, hit three times at close range,
hemorrhaging to death, Burleigh would even have noticed
the soldier. I think my own agony of pain, had I been him,
would have occupied my mind so that I would not have
even known there was anyone there to be forgiven. Then I
saw that forgiveness is only one of the attributes of love. It
is impossible to love and not forgive. Love is a fruit of the
Spirit. It just flows from a heart in which Christ abides.

Just a short distance from my grandmother's house, when
I was a child, was an artesian well which had been capped
to flow through a big pipe. I loved to go down to the well,
and watch the water gush out of a hole in the side of the
pipe at about the level of my shoulder. I would put out my
hands and feel the water rushing over them. I would stretch
out my feet and legs to be cooled in the water. No one said,
"Turn off that faucet." In fact, I managed to get wet all over
as buckets of water poured out over me. I can still remember
how free and relaxed I felt. I'd try to hold my hand over
the hole, but I couldn't stop the flow. The abundance of
the supply refused to be rationed out.

The love of God is like this artesian well. Jesus had told

the Samaritan woman at the well that anyone who believed in Him would have living water—"the water that I shall give him shall be in him a well of water springing up into everlasting life" (John 4:14, KJV). It is the springing up of this water that fills a heart and washes away an unforgiving spirit. This is what I had experienced after Burleigh's death.

Forgiveness comes naturally by God's love just as God forgives us. I do not think Christ had to strain to pray, "Father, forgive them." This was just the natural, normal response of His love. He could not have done otherwise. Love compels.

"Virginia, I do my best to try and love John," a bitter, unhappy wife said to me one day. I looked at her strained, sad face and knew that no matter how hard she was trying, she wasn't succeeding.

"Don't you know that when you're tryin' you ain't lovin'?" I said to her. "Have you ever had anyone try to love you?" Slowly she began to see my point.

I can remember some people who tried to love me. I can still see the sickly smile spread all over their faces—so thin I could see through it. I can still feel my reflex action recoil from their forced efforts to be nice and the memory is all the more painful because I can remember the open arms and warm hearts of persons who really loved me without any forced efforts.

Love is the fruit of God's Spirit abiding in our hearts. "As the branch cannot bear fruit of itself, except it abide in the vine; no more can ye, except ye abide in me. I am the vine, ye are the branches: He that abideth in me, and I in him, the same bringeth forth fruit: for without me ye can do nothing" (John 15:4-5, KJV).

Let's be honest. There are individuals that we find difficult to love. We often feel condemned because we think we should love everyone. We try our hardest. We invite them to our social functions when we really don't want them. We respond to their invitations when we really would rather not. Our sense of guilt becomes a goad in our backs to try harder.

But when we see love not as something we do but as an act of God through us, then we can be honest. "Father, I don't love him. He irritates me. I can't love him on my own but I present myself to You. I am willing for Your love to pour through me." Imagination is a marvelous gift. Just seeing yourself as a channel through which God's love flows through your head, filling your heart, and out through your face and hands, will create in you an emotion of acceptance and understanding. Whether you love this person but don't like him is no longer an issue. It is God's love which becomes your supply and it is His love you pass on.

One morning after a strenuous weekend, I was standing in line to board an airplane, not paying any particular attention to anything. Suddenly, I heard from directly in front of me, "Excuse me, but does this airplane go to Columbus?"

I looked up to discover that a lady in her late fifties was addressing me. "Why, I don't know," I said, as I looked for the flight board. I noticed that Columbus was listed. "Yes, I see it is listed. But, if you'll ask the man there in the blue suit, he'll know for sure."

As I answered her question, I observed that there were nine people behind me in line. Turning to a gentleman standing in front of me, I said, "Why did she ask me? Do I look like I know where this airplane is going?"

Before he could reply with more than a smile, our line began to move. On board the plane, however, he sat by me. He was a highly trained industrial psychologist and my experience with the lady had interested him. He shared with me his interest in the experiments being done in extrasensory perception. Although there are only experiments with no proven data at this point, I found the thoughts he gave me as a possibility so interesting, that they have continued to stick in my mind forcefully.

As I understand his explanation, many psychologists believe that every person has within his personality a "psychic radar." This operates in his subconscious mind, completely uncontrolled by any conscious effort. The biblical proverb, "as he thinketh in his heart, so is he . . ." came to my mind as he explained this (Prov. 23:7, KJV).

Each person's radar is constantly sending out its signals, expressing the reality of that person. But it is also receiving signals. Again, this is not controlled by our conscious mind, but is more a reflex action based upon that hidden personality.

"You are a Christian, aren't you?" he asked.

"Yes, I am, but what does that have to do with it?"

"I have observed that people who seem free to receive signals from others are most often Christians," he said. Then he explained, "That lady didn't really need to know about the airplane. Almost certainly she could read the sign. But flying is frightening to some people, and she needed someone to affirm her presence—someone who recognized that she was on the plane. She did not, herself, realize what she needed. But, as she passed those nine people, she was sending out a signal. From each she got a rejection signal.

"Then, when she came to you, she got a reception," he explained. "She had no idea as to whether or not you knew the answer. She only knew you would receive her."

How fascinating! Yet perhaps there was another explanation, I reasoned. She must have seen my face—I must have been remembering something pleasant.

Hardly a week later I was going to Birmingham and stopped over in Atlanta to shop. I was in a department store looking for a special kind of pin for my best dress and was leaning over carefully studying the display of pins on the counter, when someone tapped my shoulder. " 'Scuse me, Ma'am," came a voice, "but do you know where the basement is?"

I turned and saw a very poorly dressed woman standing behind me. "Well, I never knew of one being upstairs," I said, smiling. She smiled. "But, I don't know how to get there."

I turned to the counter and asked the saleslady for directions, then I repeated the instructions to my inquirer. "Do you need me to go and show you the way?" I asked.

"No, thank you," she said. "I think I can find it."

I watched her until she reached the stairs, and then I turned back to my pin selection. Suddenly it dawned upon me what had actually happened. "Thank you, Father. It even operates from the rear."

I was so excited over this thought that I shared it the next day when I spoke in Birmingham. After my talk a lovely, vivacious lady came toward me smiling. When she got about three feet away she lifted one hand, tapped her middle finger and thumb in quick taps, and said with a laugh, "Beep, beep, beep, beep."

Yet, how exciting this is! We may never know for sure, but just the thought that we could be God's radar system, sending forth His message of love is thrilling. But how wonderful to know that, although this comes from deep within me, it is not my idea or my effort. It is just the love of God going forth. Is this what II Corinthians 5:14 means by "The love of Christ controls us. . ." (RSV) or, as J. B. Phillips puts it, "The very spring of our actions is the love of God. . ."?

It is this love of God that we see so clearly in Christ. Just at the very moment when Judas departed into the night, Jesus spoke, "Oh, my children, I am with you such a short time! You will look for me, and I have to tell you as I told the Jews, 'Where I am going, you cannot follow.' Now I am giving you a new command—love one another. Just as I have loved you, you must love one another. This is how all men will know that you are my disciples, because you have such love for one another" (John 13:33-35, Phillips).

Could the world see the love in the hearts of the disciples? Not really, but they could see the fruits of this love in their relationship to each other. What would have happened had they gone forth to tell what Judas had done, their hearts filled with ill will? Judas is mentioned only a few times by the Gospel writers, and these seem incidental to the main point. I believe that it was the complete forgiveness which Christ had, because the love of God was complete in Him, that gave this command its ring of authority.

Love cannot be hid—but neither can bitterness. I once spent several days with a lady whose experience and heartbreak had left its mark of bitterness. I could see this in the way she treated others around her. There was a sag about her mouth creating a look of hardness which her expensive makeup did not hide. Even her laugh seemed sarcastic. Slowly, she began to share with me her heartbreak.

There were reasons for her bitterness. Maybe this made it harder to forgive. Yet I hurt as I realized what her unforgiving, unloving spirit had done to her. "You'll just have to forgive," I told her.

"Nobody has ever asked me to forgive," she said defensively. She had interpreted Christ as meaning that only when someone asked for forgiveness were you to forgive. If someone continued to hurt you and acted as if this were his privilege—as though your hurt was not his concern—then you were not to forgive.

There was no reason to argue with her and I was not sure that I could. Even if I gave her scriptural proof she would not hear. Yet my own distress at her misery compelled me to say, "You just must find some way to forgive."

"I don't want to forgive," she barked at me in her pain.

For a long time I sat thinking, and she quieted down. Then in deep concern I said, "You have two choices. You may either find forgiveness, or live in bitterness the rest of your life."

I looked at her carefully groomed face. Nothing was really noticeable except her bitterness. "If you don't really want to forgive," I added, "then stop wasting money on makeup. There are no cosmetics in this world that will hide bitterness."

She sat stunned at first. Then slowly, what I had said dawned upon her.

When I saw her again, a couple of years later, she was a different person. She had found forgiveness.

If an unforgiving spirit only affected the person harboring it, it might not be so bad. But it doesn't. It spreads out, contaminating those we do love. We've heard of the feuds of the McCoys and Hatfields—generations have continued to fight it without knowing why. I have found that forgiveness also bears its fruits in those we love.

While we were living in Nashville, twelve-year-old Margaret Ann was attending public school. She often came home distressed because a little girl near her own age had been very vicious toward Negroes. She had spit on the Negro woman who served in the cafeteria. Another day she had hit at the Negro maid in the wash room. Each incident distressed Margaret Ann greatly. The child had been disciplined and Margaret Ann had suffered with her in that, too.

For several weeks she had been disturbed by the girl's disrespectful acts. The child finally kicked the Negro man who had helped at the bus-loading docks. Margaret Ann came in that day really upset and she told me about the incident. Then she added, "Do you know what, Mother? A Negro hit her Daddy and killed him."

As I looked at my own bright-eyed girl, I realized that it had never occurred to her that the face of the man who killed her daddy was black. The love which flowed out in forgiveness had flowed for years in love to the Congolese. This would eternally be a part of her own life.

"To forgive is divine" was never better illustrated for

me than by a widow whose husband was killed on a trip which was purported to be a business trip but was actually a weekend trip with another woman. As she shared with me her agony and humiliation, I could not conceive of any greater grief for a wife to experience. But when she told of finding God's love real only when she forgave, I could see how divine forgiveness is. "How grateful I am," she said, "that I had to forgive in order to find God's love which I so desperately sought. If God had settled on any other terms I would have carried that burden the rest of my life."

Yet often the greatest pain in grief is being unable to forgive oneself. I'm sure a person facing the most tragic grief I have ever seen was the lady who came asking me, "Can you contact the dead?"

"Why do you want to contact the dead?" I asked.

Then she explained she and her husband had had a big misunderstanding. As he went out of the house, her final words were, "I don't care if you never come back." He had not returned.

Now she was tormenting herself, and her friends were concerned—they had never seen anyone in such inconsolable grief. She had never shared with them her haunting fear that their fuss had caused her husband to be careless. Now she lived continually with the memory of her parting words!

It was only when she realized that she needed God's forgiveness for a spirit that would express itself in such a selfish way, that she began her trek out of grief. Then she could forgive herself.

When I meet people who just can't seem to accept grief, I often find that they are harboring the memory of an incident for which they cannot forgive someone else or themselves. I often wonder how much of what appears to be deep heartbreak that can't heal or be consoled is in reality hurt that the mourner refuses to forgive, by letting God's love cleanse the heart.

Bitterness becomes most evident when others are happy. I realized to what extent God's love had healed our wounds on our first Christmas after Burleigh's death—a time I had dreaded. My family wanted us to join them, yet I felt their sympathy and efforts to make us happy would create an abnormal situation. We decided to stay in our own home, and invited two missionary friends of my sons to join us.

Shortly before Christmas vacation David and Paul informed me that David would decorate the Christmas tree and Paul would lead our Christmas morning devotions around the lighted tree. Both of these had been Burleigh's traditional responsibilities. It took great effort for me to carry on just as if everything were as usual.

I cooked a big Christmas dinner. Margaret Ann decorated the table. David played host. Sitting down to eat, we bowed our heads and David prayed.

"Father, we thank Thee for everything that has come into our lives in 1964 that has taught us the real meaning of peace on earth, goodwill to men."

He prayed on but I didn't hear it. I sat remembering the kind of world over which those angels sang. It was not a great deal different from Congo. Those shepherds heard that glorious message in spite of the strife and discord in the world of their day. They went to worship the newborn King, and to rejoice in the good news, when they could have sat in sullen bitterness and said, "What peace? Bah!"

Yes, Father, I prayed silently, *we do thank you. Help us always to remember the meaning of good will to every man— that good will begins with forgiveness.*

XII.

✐

A NEW DIMENSION OF
SERVICE

Burleigh and I once visited a lace factory in Belgium. Elderly nuns sat before small frames weaving beautiful lace in a dimly lighted room. Before each one lay a large pattern to be copied. Just about even with each nun's forehead, hung a small lamp which cast a sharp beam of intense light onto the pattern.

As I stood directly behind a nun, I observed that she could see only that part of the pattern revealed by this light. Day after day she sat weaving only that pattern she could see. Some places appeared heavy and dull, others were light and delicate, yet all of these were a part of the exquisite lace cloth, so expensive only royalty or the wealthy could ever afford it.

Many times after Burleigh died I remembered this scene and took courage. It was impossible for me to know where I was going because from the beginning I realized that God was leading me out into a new and different life. I tried not to hark back to what I had been but to look out to what I was to become. This was not easy.

As I now look back, I can see a pattern emerging which I could not see at the time. Then, I only knew that I wanted to do some type of church-related work. Teaching school did not really interest me. A master's degree in Christian education seemed to offer the best springboard into any number of avenues of service so I chose that as my major.

Then I began to write my book. Between writing and getting my degree, I did not have time to worry about where I was going or what I would do later. Yet, without my realizing it, another very definite pattern was appearing in the future design of my life.

About six month's after I started school, I received an invitation to speak at the Women's Society of Christian Service of West End Methodist Church in Nashville, Tennessee. This was my first invitation to speak, and since I expected only a few ladies, I accepted. The meeting passed without incident; I spoke and then went home, not having done anything outstanding as far as I could see. But the next morning I received a phone call.

"Would you come back again and speak for us?" It was Dr. Ben St. Clair, pastor of West End.

"Why, yes, I guess so," I replied.

We discussed a date and I accepted it. At this point I thought this would be a Sunday school class or small Sunday evening fellowship group.

"What time do you want me?" I asked.

"Eleven o'clock Sunday morning," Dr. Ben answered.

I was shocked! I had never spoken at a Sunday morning service except at First Methodist Church in Atlanta and then only on the spur of the moment shortly after Burleigh's death. The church had supported us and it was like speaking to our big family. But West End was different! It was the big university church whose members were professors at Vanderbilt and important professional people of Nashville.

"I can't do that! I wouldn't have any idea what to say."

"I want you to give as nearly as possible the same talk you gave to our W.S.C.S.," he said.

Very reluctantly I agreed. This seemed like only an isolated incident in the new pattern of my life, but it was far from it.

That Sunday morning the church was filled. Many came out of curiosity to see what kind of strange creature was this first woman to occupy the pulpit of West End Church. Others came with real interest in me and my story. Among these was a large group of delegates to a conference of jurisdictional officers for the Woman's Society of Christian Service which was meeting that weekend in Nashville. The delegates had come from all over the nation.

Less than two weeks later I was flooded with invitations to speak in churches. I was amazed! What had seemed an insignificant invitation to speak to a ladies' group had opened a floodgate of opportunities.

These opportunities came just as I had just received my last salary check from the board of missions. Although Peachtree Road Methodist Church in Atlanta was giving me a monthly scholarship payment, and the board would continue child support for my children, I had to find some kind of work. Now these invitations flooding in seemed a better answer. I could fly out on Saturday, speak on Sunday, and return early on Monday morning in time to study. I could also do collateral reading on my trips. With such a regular weekly schedule, I would be free to really study when I was home—I would not have to do outside work since my chances to make enough to support us were good. And since the whole venture would only be temporary, I would try it for about three months.

Every invitation I accepted, however, brought twice as many more. The three months stretched through the rest of the summer and into the next school year, and still every weekend I was away speaking somewhere.

Late fall came and with it calls and letters offering me numerous jobs as director of Christian education in various churches. There seemed to be a real shortage in that field—I could take my pick of ten good jobs in top churches. With these came invitations for more speaking engagements—taking me even beyond the end of the school year in June. And I had long before filled my calendar through June. That posed a problem. Still feeling homesick for Congo, and knowing that door was closed, I wanted to go overseas and was looking at Japan as a possibility. Yet here were all these other opportunities—so many I could hardly think clearly.

At this point I discovered that the wonderful sense of God's guidance that had brought me to Nashville was creating my problem. I thought I understood just how God guided. But I didn't. As soon as I thought I knew what to do, God would always seem to change the plans. I began to pray for His guidance. I honestly wanted to know and do God's will. I was sure He had a plan for me and that I would find it. Just any day I would get that glorious sense of revelation—"This is My way, walk in it." But it didn't come.

At first it didn't matter too much. Then I began to feel uneasy. And every job offer, every invitation to speak, every decision of my friends to accept a position, only added to my uneasiness.

The concept of being "clay in the potter's hands" may convey a very beautiful poetic image. We see ourselves as clay being whirled around and around on a wheel until finally the perfect vase comes forth. But the clay has no choice in the decision to mold it. As much as I might like to think of myself as clay, I wasn't. All these open doors created a pressure for decision. I had feelings and wishes. Were these of God or were they hindering my answer?

This became a period of real agony as I prayed for guidance. Yet the heavens seemed as brass. Then, very dimly at first—the thought was so terrifying—came the impression, "God isn't going to tell you what to do as He did in 1964. He isn't taking away from you the challenge of making decisions within His will." I had to learn that God only rarely speaks in a way that can't be misunderstood.

At the same time I discovered that I had no personal experience in discerning God's will in big decisions. Until I was married at nineteen, my parents had been there to take the greater responsibility. Then there was Burleigh. He and I had prayed about our decisions. I had always felt that Burleigh appreciated and wanted my ideas. If we agreed, that seemed the thing to do. If we disagreed, we would pray again, and for some time, until a decision had to be reached. Then Burleigh would decide, "This is God's will." Even though I might not fully agree, I would not object. There had never been a time when I felt that Burleigh had been totally wrong. But it had never occurred to me to ask him how he knew what was God's will.

Now I needed to know how one decided what God's will was, and I needed help desperately. I sought out a professor in whom I had great confidence. Very wisely he asked, "What are your alternatives?"

"I can be a director of Christian Education," I said, listing my job offers. "I can go to Japan and teach English and French in a girls' school. Margaret Ann could go with me. Or, I can accept all these invitations to speak."

"It seems to me," he said, "that these first two alternatives will remain open. Whether you go this year or next will not make a great deal of difference. The doors won't close so soon."

This I knew was true.

"But these speaking engagements you must accept now. If you become a director of Christian Education or go into teaching, this other door will close."

I could see this would certainly be the case.

"So why not try the speaking for just one year?" the professor went on. "If you like it and can support your family, fine! If not, then you can return to either of these other alternatives."

Although I did not have any great feeling of exhilaration at the thought of deciding to go on speaking, it did seem like good, sensible advice. With my book coming off the press in a few months, I might also want to be free to help publicize it. I wrote definitely refusing the director of Christian education jobs but telling the pastors I would try the speaking tour for one year and that I might be available after that time. I also began to fill my calendar. Long before I graduated in June, I was booked for the next year.

As soon as I received my degree in June, I moved to Wilmore, Kentucky, so that David could stay at home and commute to the University of Kentucky. Paul was in Asbury College just up the street. Margaret Ann would have her brothers at home while I traveled. Everything seemed fine as the fall plans progressed. But a new problem began to arise. I reached the point where I could not tolerate that bunch of missionary talks one more time.

Everywhere I went I was booked as a missionary. The Methodist Commission on Missions sponsored me. "Missionary Speaks" they advertised me, and worse, they always mentioned in their introduction what my coming would mean for the church's missionary emphasis. There was no question that my contribution was my missionary life and vision.

The rate at which my invitations increased—always keeping me booked for more than a year ahead—should have been all the encouragement that I needed. But it wasn't. Neither were the letters of sincere appreciation which the churches sent me after my visit. No matter what, I could not stand those talks another time.

I began to feel as if I were a tape recorder. Push a button

and out would come the same story over and over and over again. It became so routine that I would suddenly awaken in the middle of a talk to ask myself, "Did I just tell that or is it my next point?"

Regardless of what others said, I had to stop that kind of speaking. About that time I heard of a church that employed a lady to work with small groups. That kind of job appealed to me. Maybe I could find such a church in the East. Having fully made up my mind to change my job, I called a friend to ask if he knew of a church seeking such a person. He listened as I told of my decision.

"Why are you really doing this, Virginia?" he asked.

"Because I can't stand my missionary talks any longer."

"I'm glad you feel that way," he said and added in a teasing voice, "I'm tired of them, too."

Then seriously he said, "I think this feeling is from God. He wants you to move on now from being a missionary to something else He has in mind."

"But I don't know what this is. Maybe this job as prayer group leader is it," I said.

"It could be, but quite frankly I doubt it. Don't you think you should let God close His doors before you start rattling another one?"

We discussed for a long time over long distance telephone just what I could do. At his advice, I decided to throw away my old talks and, in prayer and meditation, make new ones on just whatever seemed to be on my mind at the time. I could use my illustrations from the missionary field, for after all, as my friend said, "They are yours and they are interesting because they are unique."

With great fear, I ventured out with my new talks. I shall never forget my very next engagement. It was a W.S.C.S. evening meeting in Frankfort, Kentucky and I spoke on the reality of God's presence. Not once did I refer to my missionary life or to Burleigh's death. Everyone seemed inspired except one lady who came to me. "I did hope you would tell about Brother Law's death," she said.

"That is in my book. You may read it there," I told her.

I think simply to encourage me, God impressed three visitors to ask me for an open date after that talk. I did get encouragement, yet I still had a terribly uncertain feeling. It seemed as if I were accepting invitations for one kind of service and doing another. It was as if a minister should be engaged to lead the singing for a revival only to announce at the first service, "I'm not leading the singing. I'm preaching now." The pastor would only be able to say, "God bless you, but we don't need a preacher. We already have one."

Adding to my sense of dishonesty was an even bigger discomfort that arose from the question, "What am I, then?" As long as I was a missionary speaker, I could fall back on my old identity. Now as I ventured out into this strange new ministry, I lost that. I wasn't a preacher. I really wasn't anything but a laywoman sharing my faith, and there was no place in the organizational structure of the church where I could feel attached. If only God would give me a sense of revelation—"a call" that I could accept—I would find the affirmation for what I was doing. I began to pray. I even fasted and prayed. But I did not find any kind of answer.

I had read the question somewhere, "Has God ever honored you with His silence?" I didn't count it any honor, but He surely gave me silence. During the ensuing weeks my concern built. Finally I was desperate. I had to feel some relief. As I prayed one morning, there came to me three tests by which I could know if it was God's will for me to continue speaking. The first proof would be if doors continued to open. I had found that, instead of being disappointed at my change of message, the pastors were pleased. As long as I was booked far enough ahead to feel secure I would plan to continue. If God wanted me in this unusual ministry then He would see that doors opened for me.

That meant that I would accept invitations as they came. I would not try to select the ones I wanted. If I could accept one, I would. But He knew I couldn't live away from home all the time. I would have to take time off to rest and be with Margaret Ann.

Secondly, God would supply my needs. I would simply trust Him. I would be as careful as I could, but I could not live this way and worry over making ends meet for my family. I would not be that poor, pitiful widow with runners in my hose. He must supply; and that, as He had promised, "according to His riches in glory" (Phil. 4:19, KJV) .

Both of these tests were important but not the most important one. Leaving Margaret Ann was my greatest concern. I did not think any Mother should leave a teenage daughter as I was having to do. I felt I had to, somehow, know that she was being cared for in my absence. David and Paul were both planning to marry. I would not feel responsible for them any longer but I had to know that Margaret Ann was not paying too dearly for my ministry.

I could check my date book and see how I was booked ahead; I could look at my bank account and see if it was balancing; but how could I tell about Margaret Ann? I did not know. Only a loving heavenly Father could figure that out. I simply asked Him for some assurance. It was only a few weeks later that He granted my request. And I must add, He has continued to reasure me by giving me one of the loveliest daughters any mother could wish to have.

Friends have asked me, "What would you have done if God hadn't given you the three indications you sought?"

I have to say, "I don't know. I would have had to face that then."

I do know people who have placed tests for God's guidance and they didn't work. I guess the first question I would have to ask in such a case would be, "Is this something I really need or something I only want?" And my second question would be, "Does the answer close the door?"

Perhaps the very agony of such a crisis is that no one can really face it for you. Friends may pray and support you, but you must come to grips with God's will yourself. Then, out of this kind of seeking your own tests come. You can never borrow from another—either tests or guidance. And, I might add, coming to such a crisis can not be rushed. I even tried that a few times, thinking that if I could quickly get desperate, God would answer. But I only increased my agony. Until I had ripened in God's sun, at His pace, I was not picked off the vine of pain.

After the agony (and I know no other word for it) of this crisis I took one deep breath. "Surely I have surrendered now. My cross should be over," I thought. And it did seem better for a while. But slowly I had to admit that although God was giving me blessings in abundance I really did not want this life away from home. Everything about it contradicted my natural desires. I loved my home. Nothing gave me the sense of satisfaction that keeping my home did. I loved to cook and to clean. I did not like being a celebrity.

Again and again I battled this. I blamed myself and condemned my lack of surrender. Every day of departure I would awake with a migraine headache which I knew was nothing but my resistance to leaving. How I looked forward to my times at home!

Near Easter 1967 I had more than two weeks free—a real treat. With David's wedding coming, I spent the time getting ready for guests. All my silver and brass were polished. The curtains were cleaned. The floors shined. The boys were there with their fiancees. We had a wonderful, happy time. Then it was all over—I had to leave again. I tried to accept the fact—and awoke *without* a headache. What a victory!

Paul came to drive me to the airport and as he carried out my bag I turned to close the door. My eyes swept across my home. How nice it looked! It seemed to reflect to me all the warmth and happiness we had enjoyed—and I broke into tears. All my heartbreak at leaving poured down my face as I tried to find my handerchief. I knew Paul had seen me, but he said nothing.

Seated in the car, I felt some explanation was necessary. "It just hurts me so to leave home," I said.

"I know it does, Mother. We've been praying for you." After a long pause he continued, "It seems to me that God permits you to be hurt to remind you that you're on His business."

What a thought! Could this be true? As I pondered it, I realized that if I did not hate so badly to leave I could feel guilty for going. My hurt certainly did not leave room for feelings of guilt. Once I was on my way the hurt left as I became busy and interested in my activities. On the other hand, if I had felt guilt at leaving home, it would have increased the longer I was gone.

For the first time I could look up and say, "For Your sake, Father." I began a very simple thing which took care of my departure headaches. The night before leaving, I would go to sleep saying, "Tomorrow I go to _____ for Jesus' sake." My first thought upon awakening in the morning was the same. Now I had made another step in my surrender. I had made it to Jesus.

But can this be really for Jesus' sake when I see so little accomplished? I wondered. I felt that if I could see great results, as I knew some lady preachers did, then I'd be sure that this was for Jesus' sake.

I once confided my feeling to a friend. "I believe you are one of God's seed sowers," she replied. When I awoke the next morning, I noticed beside my bed a small plaque with a Chinese proverb; "Today's flowers were yesterday's seeds."

I didn't know it then, but I had started another painful step in surrender. I felt that if I was really doing God's

will, then I should realize that I was being used. I spoke.
I shared. I listened to hundreds of problems. I went home.
Others told me I had helped their church, and pastors
recommended me to other pastors. Most of my invitations
came this way. Yet, I did not see my fruit. To be a seed
sower may sound great, but I wanted more than that.

One day I heard a Bible teacher say, "God did not call
the children of Israel to success, but to obedience."

Somehow these words burned themselves into my heart.
Success? Was that really what I called fruit? Was success
what I was seeking? Was it really always an aim of mine?

"Obedience won't be so difficult," I decided, "if I know
really what I am expected to do." Still, I did not even see
but one portion of God's pattern for me. It was go, share,
come home—week after week without seeing where this
might be leading. Then, very suddenly I realized, "I can't be
obedient, except in the very moment I am living. No matter
what I may say about obeying God tomorrow, I can't do this
until tomorrow comes." Then I not only gave up my drive
for success but I also accepted God's guidance for each step
of the way.

Obeying and enjoying obeying, however, are not always
the same thing. And I did not realize how desperately I
wanted off my circuit, until God showed me through an
experience still too painful to relate. Then I said to a close
friend, "God has either got to change me or change this
circuit."

Even as I said it, I had a vague, uneasy feeling as to
which would change. My battleground was fast becoming
my lack of a "call." In the past there had been times when
I had known definitely that God had revealed to me the
way I should go. I knew He *could* say, "Here it is," and I'd
have the assurance that what I was doing was His definite
will. But this time no "call," no revelation came.

I felt trapped. I thought of doing something else. I certainly felt better qualified for other things, but how could I just pick out another job on my own. I'd be worse off then. At least these doors had been opened for me. I didn't open them myself.

During these days three hints were dropped to me. Speaking of a very successful preacher, a friend, said, "God has called him to this special ministry and he pushes down the doors to do it."

Another friend, telling of a young man who had sold his business to enter the ministry, remarked about his dramatic call, "I don't believe he could have obeyed without such a call."

Then a letter came to me from a friend saying, "I marvel at the miracle of your open doors."

These three incidents had no relation at all, until one morning when the Holy Spirit connected them for me.

Remembering the young man, I heard a very personal question, "Can't you be obedient without some dramatic revelation?" Then I realized that everywhere I went I was urging people just to be obedient, day by day; "just do what God shows you at the moment." Such excellent advice! Only with shame did I realize that I did not want to follow it. "Why do you want some special revelation?" I heard the question so strongly.

"I really don't have a good reason," I had to admit.

"Then, can you be obedient?" I had to face this question. It demanded an answer!

"I don't really want to," I had to say honestly, "but I will." And I meant it.

Then comments came to me, recalling my friend who pushed down his doors. "Which would you rather have—your open door or God's call?"

"No doubt about that—my open doors."

I have since come to believe that the positiveness of God's revelation is in direct relationship to the difficulty of execution. He never gives a clear "call" that is easy to answer.

Then, the miracle of these open doors really dawned upon me for the first time. After months of agonizing and seeking, I could say with confidence, "God has not called me, but He has led me into this strange new life."

I had often heard Christians say that when you truly come to want God's will, then you come to enjoy it. I had heard witnesses tell how they had fought God's call, only to surrender and find it their supreme joy. I hated to admit it, but I had not found this to be true. Something must yet be wrong with my surrender.

This time I was not left long in my agony. Just about the time I admitted that I wasn't happy doing God's will, I had an opportunity to talk with one of God's true saints. "Should I find real joy in doing this if I'm truly surrendered?" I asked.

"Why, no," he answered. "God has called you to bear a cross. If you enjoyed a cross you'd be psychotic. You can rejoice in obedience, not in the cross."

I guess I had considered my loss of Burleigh as my cross, but suddenly I realized it was not. Why would Jesus put an "if" in front of His call to discipleship ("If any man will come after me, let him . . . take up his cross, and follow me"—Matt. 16:24, KJV), if no choice were offered? I had no choice in giving up Burleigh. Leaving my home and my loving daughter was obviously my cross because every time I left, I knew I didn't really have to. Many jobs I could do would permit me to stay at home.

Then, finally, I surrendered; I reached down and accepted my cross in order to follow Jesus. The moment I made that step, I knew that my battle for finding and accepting God's will was won. My heart was at peace as it had never really been since Burleigh's death.

I felt like a ball that had bounced around and finally rolled into a soft, velvet pocket.

"But why did it take me so long?" I wondered. My desire to do God's will was no keener at this point than it was two years before when I had started seeking it. I had surrendered then as best I could. My heart did not reject this conviction.

Then it came to me. "It isn't a surrender when an army raises their white flag; no matter how serious they are. The surrender comes when every arm has been laid down and they accept a new master."

It had taken me two long years to lay down my arms and take up my cross to follow Jesus.

XIII.

∽

AS FAR AS I CAN STEP

THERE IS A CARTOON pinned to the lampshade by my bed. It comes from my favorite cartoon strip, "Peanuts." Linus meets Lucy. "What do you do when something doesn't happen when you were so sure it would?" he asks.

"Well, you could admit that you were wrong," she answers.

"Besides that, I mean," Linus says.

There are just too many times when I think I've figured out exactly what God is doing, or going to do, only to discover I am wrong.

The morning of a speaking engagement I awoke barely able to speak. It was most obvious that I had a severe case of laryngitis. Naturally I was distressed—laryngitis is a public speaker's nightmare! I prayed for guidance. Once before I had experienced a real miracle. That time God had miraculously touched my voice at the last minute, and I had spoken clearly. I believed He could do the same again.

As I prayed, I felt no positive direction. Should I go

ahead? Or should I cancel? Then I followed a suggestion I
had picked up somewhere. In my imagination I pictured
myself going, then staying. I waited a moment for that impression to clear and repeated it in reverse order: staying,
then going. There was no question about it. I felt uneasy at
the thought of staying but comfortable at the thought of
going. I prepared to go.

All day I made positive affirmations for my healing. I
thanked God that He was healing me. And He was, but not
fast enough for a 7:30 speaking engagement. By five o'clock
I began to be distressed. It was pretty evident that, if anything, I was worse. I went alone to pray.

My first reaction was that I had just plain been mistaken
in my guidance. Yet as I prayed, I couldn't seem to feel any
condemnation. Was I supposed to be healed? I had expected
it, but if this was the answer, some angel needed to get busy.
As I prayed the thought came, "You have a tape of a talk;
use it."

True enough, I did have in my suitcase a tape of a talk
which I no longer gave. I could use that if I had to. I took
it down to the pastor. He still had faith for my healing but
we agreed to be prepared.

The service began. The pastor introduced me. I rose to
speak but not a clear sound came forth. We started the tape
recorder while I pulled up a chair. I sat there and heard
myself give my talk.

Early the next morning I lay in bed thinking, "Gee, I
sure missed that time."

Then, so clearly, I seemed to hear, "Not really. You only
misunderstood the purpose of your coming." Very strangely
the Spirit revealed to me that He had sent me there for a
reason that had nothing to do with my speaking. No one
else may know why I went but I do.

This made me realize more than ever that I am a part of
God's ideas and plans, not He of mine. I may not realize

what He is doing, but if I am obedient to the best I can know, then the results are His responsibility, not mine.

Part of His wonder is His ability to reveal Himself to me. I found, to my amazement, that I trusted God's plans in everything but in Virginia. I could believe that God sent me towels when I needed them. I could see His hand in external matters, but I was not so sure of His part if I were to be involved—I knew Virginia too well.

The day for my trip to the Minnesota Conference Convocation of Methodist Men came and with it a terrible snow that cancelled all flights into Chicago. I, along with hundreds of other passengers, was stranded in Cincinnati. Every airline gave me the same answer, "There's no way to reach Minneapolis except through Chicago."

Discouraged, I went into the dining room for lunch. As I waited for my waitress, I lifted my heart in prayer. "Father, if You want me in Minnesota, You will not only have to make it possible but will have to tell me what to do. No one else seems to know of any way."

The waitress came and I gave her my order. Just so naturally my mind began to wander. *When did I eat that salad before? I remember it was real good. When was I here last? Oh, yes, I remember, I flew here from Pittsburg on a TWA plane going to St. Louis.*

When my mind reached St. Louis I felt the compelling urge, "Fly to St. Louis."

I asked the waitress to hold my salad and I rushed out to TWA. They could only give me a stand-by reservation but the agent stamped my ticket 11:45 A.M. I went back, ate my lunch and then called Minnesota. The program chairman urged me to go ahead and try for St. Louis. At least I would be on the back side of the storm. They were having beautiful weather so maybe I could get up from St. Louis. Besides, I was one of their main speakers. It would be very difficult for them to find a replacement so late.

At three o'clock I went out to the gate. A gentleman sitting next to me had 11:47 stamped on his ticket. He held a confirmed reservation for later but was afraid the storm might close in. One by one the stand-by passengers were called. A few went out. A few more were called. They stopped calling. It appeared that the plane was filled. Then, one more call: "Mrs. Law."

I was the last passenger to board that plane. My two-minute advantage put me ahead of the gentleman who had a reservation later. What if I had argued with my inspiration for 3 minutes?

But in St. Louis, I still couldn't get reservations to Minneapolis. Not even a stand-by was promised. Again I called the program chairman. "Just go on to bed and get a good night's rest. I have your phone number. We'll see what God does provide."

Early the next morning he called again. "Go out to St. Louis Air Taxi at 11:30," he said. "Watkin's Company is sending its VIP plane down for you."

Promptly at 11:30 a beautiful new Cessna 310 flew in. I climbed in and flew from St. Louis in real style. It all worked out so perfectly that it became a very exciting experience. Yet, as I looked back, I found one question persisting in my mind, "How did God guide you?"

I had to admit that it was my mind that received the thoughts. It was natural that I had been thinking about my last salad. Then, remembering how I came there, God was using just my normal processes of thought to bring His special guidance. How else does He really have to speak to me except through my mind? Here is where my thoughts are formulated—"it is God who is at work within you, giving you the will and the power to achieve his purpose" (Phil. 2:13, Phillips). If I were going to know this will which God was working then I would have to trust Him to work in me.

As I tried to trust confidently, I had an opportunity to

be near a Christian friend whom I trusted. I shared a thought that I had had about our meeting. He sat for a moment thinking and then said, "I feel comfortable with that idea." He had a confidence in the Holy Spirit that I envied. Yet, as I sought to grow, I finally found that this was the guidance I too trusted; if I felt comfortable about it, I proceeded; if I felt uncomfortable, I waited. And yet, could you always trust your feelings? I could not help but see people who seemed to do the most foolish things under what they called "guidance." I found, once again, that I was trying to stretch my faith and my experiences to cover other people, and this simply could not be done. I would have to find God's revelation for myself and learn to recognize His voice, but I would have to trust this power within my own mind and heart.

These impressions were often a feeling of heaviness when I was on the wrong route. Yet I learned that God dealt in specifics. This heaviness was not a depression of undefined misery. When I stopped to seek direction, the heaviness moved away. Again, my impression was a lift of the Spirit— a feeling of excitement as I considered some plan. Again, it could be a deep desire I felt within my heart.

In trying to recreate a home, I had, from time to time, collected pieces of antique glass for a bay window I hoped to have some day. It was a slow process, but I had come to see a real possibility that this bay window might not be too far away. I began watching more carefully for items I could add to my collection.

I was traveling one hot afternoon and felt sleepy. To break the monotony of driving, I stopped along the road at various "Antique Shoppes" but saw nothing that interested me. I was nearing my destination when I saw a very small sign. There was time for one more look, so I turned around and drove back into the yard where the sign stood. There was a small shop in what had been the single-car garage of a small white frame house. I tried the door of the shop but it was locked. No one was at home. I peered in the window. There on the shelf sat a pretty little red ruby glass pitcher with a white cut glass bottom. It looked just like one the rebel soldiers had looted from my Congo home. I stood looking at it, imagining it once more in my front window with the light shining through. But the shop was closed. I couldn't get it. Dismissing it from my mind, I drove on to my Friday evening meeting.

The next morning as I was meditating and praying, this little pitcher suddenly appeared right in the midst of my devotional thoughts. I pushed this disturbing intrusion from my mind and concentrated harder on my prayers. When I had finished praying I checked to see if this shop was listed in the phone book, but could find no listing.

Sunday morning I again found the little ruby pitcher disturbing my thoughts. "This is strange," I thought. "I don't usually want something like that so badly." Several times during Sunday it came to my mind.

Then Monday morning as I was preparing to leave, the vase was there again—I wanted it. "It must be because it reminds me of Congo," I reasoned as I tried to dismiss the thought.

But the thought refused to be dismissed. I seemed compelled to go back the few miles out of my way to see about it. As I drove I couldn't help but wonder about this compelling desire to get that piece of antique glass. Could this be the Holy Spirit guiding me?

I began to construct some explanation, for I knew this was not my usual reaction to buying something. "Maybe the pitcher is real cheap and I can buy it for next to nothing. It will pay me to drive the extra miles for such a bargain," I mused.

The shop was open when I got to it, but no one was there. Sure enough, my little glass pitcher was just what I had hoped it was. I picked it up and examined it carefully, but there was no price on it. Putting it down, I looked around. There on a table was a small white cut glass bowl— I wanted it too.

The door opened and a young lady came in. I showed her the two pieces. "How much are they?" I asked.

"Twenty dollars for the two" she answered.

Goodness me, I thought. *That sure isn't any bargain, Father.*

I turned my back to the owner as if looking at something else but I was praying. *Now that isn't a bargain. I don't see how I can afford them. Maybe I'll just get the little pitcher.*

"How much is the pitcher by itself?" I asked.

"Ten dollars."

Again I walked over to the pitcher. *I'll just get this. It isn't any bargain but I'll only be wasting half as much money,* I reasoned silently.

But suddenly a heavy sense of burden rolled over my heart. *Father, I don't understand this,* I prayed. *Could You be telling me to splurge twenty dollars on something I don't really need? Now if this is not of Your Spirit take it away. If it is from You, then make it so strong I can't resist.*

I waited a moment. There was no question. I had to buy those two pieces of antique glass. I turned to the owner and said, "I'll take them."

She began wrapping them up. As she finished the bowl, a little girl, about three years of age, wearing a leg brace came in. The mother smiled at her and then said to me, "This really is an answer to prayer."

"How's that?" I asked.

"My little girl here was born crippled. It cost so much to treat her, we just couldn't keep up with the bills," she hesitated a moment, then continued, "I don't know about you, but me and my husband are Christians. We prayed for God to open up some way that I could stay home and still help earn enough for her medical bills."

Again she hesitated as if fearful I might not understand. "God answered our prayers. I inherited some antiques so we closed in this garage for a little shop. For two years I've made enough to keep up my stock and pay her bills. We don't spend this for anything else, but this money has run out. She needs to have a kidney irrigation this morning and I didn't have the twenty dollars."

"When did you know she'd need this?" I asked.

"Friday afternoon," she said. Then added, "But Saturday is usually my best day so I wasn't worried until I didn't sell one thing on Saturday."

"I guess that did bother you," I said.

"Not really until this morning. After my husband went to work and I saw I still didn't have the money, I did all I knew to do—I prayed. I asked God to send me somebody to buy twenty dollars worth of antiques before ten o'clock."

I looked at my watch. It was ten minutes to ten.

"I knew it was Monday and not a good day for sales, but I needed help and I believed He could answer. I went ahead and dressed my little girl to go."

When I told her how I happened to be there, I cried and she cried. "This is an example of His promise, 'Before you call I will hear and while you are yet speaking I will answer,' " I said.

As I drove away, the marvel of such a miracle gripped me. God had given me this desire for an antique vase— this was not my own selfish urge to buy something. I was a part of His answer to this child of His, but she was also an avenue of a continual joy to me. Each time I look at the glass I remember.

I soon discovered that God did not give me any revelation that was contradictory to His Word. Yet I was amazed to find how often in reading His Word I discovered the message I needed. Suddenly an often-read passage seemed to come alive. The more I read, the greater hunger I had to really know what the Scriptures had to say to me. I now feel a real spiritual thirst and hunger to read my Bible.

My capacity to know God's guidance seems to depend upon my obedience. "We receive whatever we ask for, because we are obeying his orders . . ." (I John 3:22, Phillips). How painful it was one day, when I could not get the directions I needed, to quietly hear, "You haven't done the last thing I told you." So true has this been that I often find myself backing up to ask myself, "Have I really obeyed?"

At other times, I not only ask, "Have I obeyed?" but "Did I really listen to hear God's guidance?" I remember that when David first got his driver's license, I came out to him, handed him the keys, and said, "David, please go . . ." and he did. Some minutes later he came in rather sheepishly. "Where did you say to go, Mother?" he asked.

"I didn't. You left before I had a chance," I told him. How often I only wait long enough to hear "Go!"

Yet, again, I have discovered that I had correctly heard God's guidance, but it was only for that moment. God does not always guide me directly to the target. An army pilot explained to me one day that in the Second World War, they never took off and flew directly to target. To trick the enemy they flew in a zig-zag pattern—so many degrees north, then so many south. Sometimes, even in flight, their orders would change. How tragic would have been the result had he replied, "No, Sir, I have my orders. I'm sticking to them." More and more I have to say, "This is my guidance for this moment. If God changes it tomorrow, then I'll do something different."

Sometimes it seems impossible to recognize just what God is trying to say. Many of my most agonizing moments have come when, seek as I may, I cannot seem to know what I should do. Then, "Put out a fleece," my friends advise.

This advice goes back to Gideon in Judges 6:33-40. The Midianites and Amalekites came against the army of Israel.

Gideon needed some real assurance that the Lord would save Israel by his leadership, as He had said. To test this guidance, Gideon put a fleece of wool on the floor. If dew wet the fleece and not the floor, then Gideon would know he was being led of God. The next morning he could wring a bowl of water out of the fleece. The floor was dry. Gideon still wasn't convinced so he changed his request and asked that, for the second testing, the fleece be dry and the floor be wet. In the morning the fleece was dry.

I hate to admit it, but some of my biggest mistakes have been in putting out fleeces. And I wouldn't have said anything if my Christian friends did not have the same confession. While a fleece may prove to be positive guidance, it cannot always be a foolproof one.

It seems to me that I must first be sure that I really need to know and am not merely wanting what amounts to clairvoyance or fortunetelling. If it is my curiosity or impatience which drives me to put out a fleece, it will most surely fail.

Secondly, the fleece must be so natural that I do not have to search to discover one. When I have difficulty in deciding how to state the two alternatives, I have learned to just drop both of them. When my fleece is truly a testing of the Spirit, to be sure it is of God, the two alternatives are very clear—I can clearly state them to a friend, or I can write them down as I place them before God. And I date my record of these requests. To me, this is very important.

If I can possibly do so, I share my burden with a friend, because this extra check helps me to avoid self-delusion. But, since at times this is not possible, my dated written statement is a help.

I shared this practice of mine with a friend who faced a question. Suddenly God had provided money and he announced this was for an idea he had been praying about. Others involved did not agree. "But," he insisted, "I told God that if He wanted this to come to pass to send exactly this amount." Yet this was the first anyone had heard of this fleece.

Time proved my friend wrong. His experience showed me again the danger of any fleece put out in secret without even a written record. What saved this friend was his willingness to say, "Okay. If God is leading, then He will continue to open the doors."

Someone has said, "We rattle the door knobs but we don't kick down God's doors." Often putting out a fleece is really asking God for more guidance than He is ready to give. But if we will begin to move, slowly by faith, God will open the door. It is difficult to steer a car that is parked with the brakes on. If they are moving slowly, even difficult people can be guided.

While traveling one day, we lost our direction in a large city, and stopped at a filling station to inquire. "Do we have to go all the way back into the city?" I asked.

"No," the man said. "There's a shortcut across to your route."

As I rode on I thought about this. How true this is in my Christian life. While trying almost too hard to find my way I would get off onto the wrong route, yet God seems to always have a shortcut to my correct route. He never sends me back to start over.

Even when I have tried to get sure direction by putting out a fleece, I have often discovered that I had to come back to my own impressions of the Spirit. I experienced this while I felt such a need to have a home. Renting was so indefinite. A place I could decorate and make mine was a very deep need. I prayed for guidance. The question as to whether or not I could get a loan seemed my best fleece. I could. I had the plans. I had the down payment. Yet every time I prayed, despite what seemed my wet fleece, I felt a negative emotion. I had no lift of the Spirit as I prayed, even though I really wanted it. After weeks of trying to decide I dropped the idea.

"When You are ready for me to have a home, Father, You just let me know," I prayed.

Months passed and I did not pray again about this. Every time I was reminded of this desire or need, I simply said, "In Your good time, Lord, I will receive this."

More than a year later, a nice, fairly new home came on the market. It was well located and within our price range. Suddenly, as definitely as I had felt "don't buy," I felt that I should buy. Again everything worked out, but this time I felt totally free and excited over the house. I began to dream of decorating it. My money was limited but I could even get excited over getting old furniture to antique or refinish. I had no hope of new pieces to add to what I had. But, one by one, from friends I did not even know the year before, pieces of lovely new furniture were made possible to me. Looking back now, I can see that my first fleece could have determined my course of action. God did not close the door. I could have gone ahead, but how much more blessed I was when I ultimately trusted His guidance of the Spirit within rather than my fleece without.

The open door can often be the best test of God's guidance. "If you want this, Father, then make it possible and give the witness of your Spirit." It is the quiet, abiding presence of His Spirit that leads us into all truth. With His eye He has promised to guide us (see Ps. 32:8) .

Yet, more than in external matters, I have felt the deep need for His presence in guiding me into His truth. When I was suddenly cast from a very isolated place of service onto center stage, I found I was constantly fearful. I realized that most of my fear came when some person came to me for help. "Who was I to be trying to help them?"

I confessed to an experienced Christian my uneasiness. She had been with me for several weeks as we worked together in witnessing to our faith. "You are adequate, by God's grace, for every opportunity He sends you—else He wouldn't have sent it," she said to me. "When the need comes, He'll give you the gifts of His Spirit," she added.

"Gifts of His Spirit?" I asked myself. "Are these the same as talents?" Strange, after all my years as a Christian I had not heard about these. I began to read and study. Paul spoke of these gifts, especially in I Corinthians 12:4-10. "Men have different gifts, but it is the same Spirit who gives them. There are different ways of serving God, but it is the same Lord who is served. God works through different men in different ways, but it is the same God who achieves his purpose through them all. Each man is given his gift by the Spirit that he may use it for the common good.

"One man's gift by the Spirit is to speak with wisdom, another's to speak with knowledge. The same Spirit gives to another man faith, to another the ability to heal, to another the power to do great deeds. The same Spirit gives to another man the gift of preaching the word of God, to another the ability to discriminate in spiritual matters, to another speech in different tongues and to yet another the power to interpret the tongues. Behind all these gifts is the operation of the same Spirit, who distributes to each individual man, as he wills" (Phillips) .

In my travels I met people who claimed to have these different gifts. They seemed to feel that God had bestowed upon them some special ability and it was theirs like a gift in a carefully guarded box. Any time they chose they could call this forth. It was theirs and always available. I wasn't sure which gift I would prefer, but I certainly did long to have this special sense of equipping for my new ministry. I had no question about the presence of the Holy Spirit in my life, but these special gifts I did not recognize. Yet, I read that we should set our hearts on the highest and best spiritual gifts (I Cor. 12:31) .

As I began to seek, I discovered to my amazement that God had been giving me these gifts all the time as I had need of them. But my gifts had been such a natural part of me that I had not recognized them.

When suddenly called upon to help people who came to me, I felt uneasy. This was responsibility that seemed overpowering and awesome. What if I said something that misled them? Then I discovered that, as I listened to a person, there would come to my mind a persistent question. Often this question would lead to another one. If I just kept asking those questions which came to my mind so persistently, the people always did one of two things. They would either suddenly get a bright look of inspiration and say, "You know, that's it. I never thought of that," or they would look distressed and break down to confess that all the time they had been lying. What amazed me was that I had not suspected a falsehood. The Spirit had revealed it.

One day a lovely young girl came to me with a marriage problem. She told me a beautiful love story. Again and again she said, "There is no one to whom I can talk about this."

She told me that she worked for a professional man, one I knew whom many people confided in. As the conversation progressed, long after her comment about her work, very suddenly came the question, "Why can't she talk with her boss?"

I asked her this only to see a horrible look of panic grip her face. She sat stunned! Then she broke down. She had been having an affair with her boss. Her husband had discovered them. Now that she had become honest we could make progress. What she really needed was a good confession.

My gift of wisdom was not in answers but in questions. Painfully I discovered that my gift is not something I can take out at will. It is not my gift but His gift, for a special need—for a special time. Sometimes, even when I thought I needed it, it didn't seem available. Then I would realize that I wanted to score 100 percent—never have to admit to failure. Only when I realize that often I am only a link in God's chain, and not even the final link, can I rest in confidence. Many times I am wonderfully blessed to be the last link leading the person to Christ. Again, I have seen that I was next to last. But again, I don't have any idea where in the chain I come. Then I can only search my heart to see if I have been faithful and obedient. If my heart does not condemn me, I rest the person in His love.

A spirit of understanding seemed more of a special gift. Once a friend of mine seemed to have a difficult problem, yet I was amazed to realize that I could somehow see through it and understand it. As I talked with her I was able to help.

A few days later a really interested friend asked me, "What's her trouble?"

"Well, I'll tell you . . ." I started to answer. Suddenly deep within I felt checked. *Oh no you don't,* I heard so clearly.

". . . I wish I really knew," I finished my sentence.

This experience frightened me. These gifts are really His, not mine. I am trusted with them only for serving Him. In fact, I cannot say I have this or that gift. I can only say, "The Holy Spirit gave me a gift to use for this special situation."

As I use His gifts I become better able to use them. I recognize them more quickly. I draw upon them with more confidence. But I also know when I have failed to use them. My successes are more precious but my failures are more painful.

Straining to exercise gifts has brought some of my greatest agonies. To live so close to God that I could know His will and affirm His purposes is an ideal to strive for, yet one of my greatest failures was in this very area. I felt I had discerned God's will in a certain situation. My fleece had been wet, then dry, so I knew exactly what would happen. I prayed, in faith, believing. I affirmed the answer. I was dead wrong! I was also spiritually crushed. For several weeks after

I could not pray—I felt as though God had let me down. I'm not sure that even yet I fully understand, but I have learned a little more.

But I have had the opposite experience also. I was in Jacksonville, Florida when I received word that my seven-year-old niece was to have surgery for a brain tumor that very morning in Gainesville. The doctors gave the family no hope. As I prayed with a group of friends, I felt a sense of utter peace. I was not even apprehensive. I simply knew that Michele would live. As we drove down to Gainesville, I remarked to a friend that I felt so confident.

As I rode the hospital elevator I asked myself, "Are you going to tell Jane?"

I remembered my recent experience of misinterpretation. But this time I wasn't *trying* to believe. I simply seemed to know! "I'd rather be faithful to my faith and be wrong, than to deny it by silence," I decided.

When I walked in the waiting room and embraced my sister, I said, "Michele is going to be all right, Jane."

Michele is a living miracle, according to her doctors. But she is to me a result of my gift of faith. It seems to me that, in the first instance, in my effort to discern God's will, I got ahead of His gift of faith. I did not have the deep abiding peace and witness. I was trying to force something into being, like trying to force an apple to grow. It didn't work—it can't be done.

As I contrast my painful failure with my glorious success, I realize I should never have tried to strain my faith. I should have rested my case with God, affirmed that He had a will, and believed that this will would be done. But until He gave me the gift of understanding just what His will really was for the situation, and His gift of faith for it, I should have done nothing. As it was, I simply messed up the situation with my own discernments.

I do believe that as a person walks with the Lord, his

understanding grows and his faith does move mountains. But that is not the goal to strive for. As I have talked with some of God's saints, I have discovered that they seek to know Christ and His will and to exercise faith in Him. Then He gives them His gift of faith. Growing in fruitfulness and in faith is on the same basis as coming to Christ. It is nothing we could or did achieve. Rather it is God's gift of grace which saves us. No one can pride himself upon earning the love of God. The fact is that what we are we owe to the hand of God upon us. "For we are his workmanship, created in Christ Jesus to do those good deeds which God planned for us to do" (Eph. 2:10, Phillips).

My friend was right. I could be adequate by God's grace for every good deed He planned for me to do. I did not have this gift or that gift but I had all His gifts that I needed for a particular ministry.

Four years after my life was shattered, I could look back and see the smiles He had given me in my tears. It was as though I had come to a lookout on a mountain and could look back over the road I had just traveled. It was very clear that God's hand had been upon me. Now my confidence would be in Him.

In Congo, we had older men who served as sentries at night. They swept the yard, heated bath water, guarded the house, and were most useful in carrying notes at night.

Going about your business in an evening, you would often hear a cough at the door. You never knew how long one of these messengers had stood there before he announced his presence. One missionary commented that a good book title would be, "What I Saw While I Waited to Cough." No doubt many secrets were learned by these men.

One night I heard a familiar cough. When I went to the door, I could just make out the figure of Papa Jean, the sentry from the single ladies' house, holding out a note. It was a dark, dark tropical night. No moon or stars were shining. There were no street lights on this isolated situation. A small six-inch kerosene lantern with a smoky chimney in Papa Jean's hand gave the only smattering of light.

Such a pitiful little light in such a dark night, I thought. "That lamp doesn't give much light, does it, Papa?" I said to him.

"No, it doesn't," he answered. "But it shines as far as I can step."

That little incident has become a symbol for my future. Looking back I can see a pattern—God did have a plan for me. Looking ahead I still can't be sure where I am going, but the years have taught me to walk with confidence. God's love always lights my path as far as I can step.